MICHIGAN'S TOWN & COUNTRY INNS

Michigan's Town & Country Inns

FIFTH EDITION

Susan Newhof

The University of Michigan Press
Ann Arbor

Published in the United States of America by
The University of Michigan Press
Manufactured in the United States of America
⊚ Printed on acid-free paper

2016   2015   2014   2013   4   3   2   1

A CIP catalog record for this book is available from the British Library.

ISBN 978-0-472-03517-5 (pbk. : alk. paper)
ISBN 978-0-472-02951-8 (e-book)

Unless otherwise indicated, photos have been provided courtesy of the respective inn.

To my dear friend
Rosanne Taylor,
with love

Ahmeek
Laurium

Big Bay

NORTH COUNTRY   Curtis

Blaney Park

St. Ignace Mackinac Island
Bois Blanc Island   ISLANDS IN THE
STRAITS

Petoskey   Bay View
Charlevoix
Walloon Lake Village   Wolverine
Leland
Suttons Bay   Bellaire
Traverse City   Old Mission Peninsula

LAND OF LITTLE BAYS

Prudenville

Ludington
Pentwater

Mount Pleasant
Jugville (White Cloud)   Bay City
Whitehall
Muskegon   Alma   Lexington
Grand Haven   HEARTLAND   SOUTHERN
SUNRISE
Grandville

Holland   Auburn Hills
Saugatuck
Allegan   Eaton Rapids
South Haven   Plymouth
SOUTHERN SUNSET   Battle Creek   Ypsilanti
St. Joseph   Kalamazoo Marshall
Union City Jonesville
Coldwater

Contents

Introduction   1

NORTH COUNTRY:
THE UPPER PENINSULA

Ahmeek
Sand Hills Lighthouse Inn   8

Big Bay
Thunder Bay Inn   11

Blaney Park
Celibeth House Bed and Breakfast   14

Curtis
Chamberlin's Ole Forest Inn   17

Laurium
*Laurium Manor Inn and
Victorian Hall Bed and Breakfast*   20

St. Ignace
The Boardwalk Inn   24

ISLANDS IN THE STRAITS:
BOIS BLANC ISLAND AND MACKINAC ISLAND

Bois Blanc Island
Insel Haus   31

Mackinac Island
Cloghaun   35
Metivier Inn   38

LAND OF LITTLE BAYS:
NORTHERN LOWER PENINSULA

Bay View
  The Terrace Inn   43

Bellaire
  Bellaire Bed and Breakfast   46
  The Grand Victorian Bed and Breakfast Inn   50

Charlevoix
  Horton Creek Inn Bed and Breakfast   54

Leland
  The Riverside Inn   57

Ludington
  Ludington House Bed and Breakfast   61
  Cartier Mansion   64

Old Mission Peninsula
  Chateau Chantal Winery and Inn   67
  The Inn at Chateau Grand Traverse   72

Pentwater
  Hexagon House   76

Petoskey
  Stafford's Bay View Inn   79

Prudenville
  Springbrook Inn   82

Suttons Bay
  The Inn at Black Star Farms   86

Traverse City
  Antiquities Wellington Inn   90

Walloon Lake Village
  Walloon Lake Inn   94

Wolverine
  Silent Sport Lodge Wilderness Bed and Breakfast   98

SOUTHERN SUNSET:
THE SOUTHWESTERN LOWER PENINSULA

Allegan
   Castle in the Country   105

Grand Haven
   Harbor House Inn   109

Holland
   Crimson Cottage in the Woods   112

Muskegon
   Port City Victorian Inn   117

St. Joseph
   South Cliff Inn   122

Saugatuck
   Belvedere Inn   126
   Wickwood Inn   130

South Haven
   Yelton Manor Bed and Breakfast   134

Whitehall
   A Finch Nest Bed and Breakfast   139
   Cocoa Cottage Bed and Breakfast   143
   White Swan Inn   147

HEARTLAND:
THE CENTRAL LOWER PENINSULA

Alma
   Saravilla Bed and Breakfast   153

Battle Creek
   Greencrest Manor   157

Coldwater
   Chicago Pike Inn and Spa   161

Eaton Rapids
   The English Inn   165

Grandville
    Prairieside Suites Luxury Bed and Breakfast   169

Jonesville
    Munro House Bed and Breakfast   173

Jugville (White Cloud)
    The Shack   177

Kalamazoo
    Kalamazoo House Bed and Breakfast   181

Marshall
    The National House Inn   185

Mount Pleasant
    Country Chalet and Edelweiss Haus   188
    Ginkgo Tree Inn   192

Union City
    The Victorian Villa Inn   196

SOUTHERN SUNRISE:
THE SOUTHEASTERN LOWER PENINSULA

Auburn Hills
    Cobblestone Manor   203

Bay City
    Chesny's Keswick Manor   207
    The Historic Webster House   211

Lexington
    A Night to Remember Bed and Breakfast   215

Plymouth
    932 Penniman   219

Ypsilanti
    The Parish House Inn   223

Resources   227

Introduction

To quote Dr. Seuss, "Oh the places you'll go!"

In the past forty years, this state has been blessed with the opening of hundreds of fine inns and bed-and-breakfast homes across both peninsulas. They come in all sizes and shapes and encompass a great variety from Queen Anne mansions to contemporary chic, urban oases to historic small-town getaways. They are tucked deep in forests and perch on islands. Some appeal to business travelers or families traveling with children. Some inspire romance. A few have everything you need for a remember-it-for-a-lifetime wedding. Several are homes built before Michigan women had the right to vote. One of my favorites was welcoming travelers before Michigan became a state!

They are as unique as snowflakes, and that, in part, is what makes them so appealing.

What they have in common is that they offer an *experience.* And they do that because you, the traveler, have said that's what you want. You say you want to make memories—good ones—of raising a glass of wine in front of a crackling fireplace, of four poster beds, sunsets and soaker tubs and perhaps a cat on your lap. You want to live, for a few days, like a lumber baron, a Victorian lady, a winemaker or a woodsman. You want to rekindle your love or get away with girlfriends, spend the day hiking, shop till you drop, dig deep into history or blow it all off with a glorious day at the beach. You want privacy or to meet other guests whose stories are as interesting as your own. You want good food and innkeepers who are warm and friendly and who happily introduce you to their corner of Michigan. And that is exactly what you'll find in these pages.

The most difficult part of this project was whittling down the list of inns for this edition from all the worthy options. To begin, I focused on inns with four rooms or more, though you will find a couple that are smaller. I looked for those incorporating environmentally friendly practices, and I asked about the ability to juggle diverse dietary needs of guests.

I looked for inns with on-site extras and discovered everything from restaurants and wineries to antique stores, spa services and great fishing out the back door. The drawing card for some is their proximity to a hip urban area. For others, it's access to winter sports. One inn starred in a movie. A few are longtime favorites, and some simply grabbed me as soon as I walked through the door. And talk about architectural variety . . . from a nineteenth-century stagecoach stop to neoclassical, English Tudor to prairie style, French Normandy to contemporary log, I found it all.

Still, because of space, I had to leave out dozens that are absolutely top-notch. To help you find them, I've listed B&B associations and other resources at the end of the book.

I am occasionally asked why I include so much information about the innkeepers, and my answer, after so many years of meeting them, remains the same: in most cases, they are the heart and soul of an inn. At smaller B&Bs, it's often in their living room that you will spend the evening chatting with other guests and in their kitchen or dining room that you will continue conversations over morning coffee. An innkeeper gives a place its flavor and sets the mood.

Some innkeepers are accomplished artists, athletes or scholars. A few have had distinguished military careers. I have met some who are quiet and pensive and others who love to engage their guests in conversations that last long into the night. Generally, the smaller the inn the greater the presence of the innkeeper.

Innkeepers tell me many of their guests become friends. Guests tell me they visit an inn for the first time, usually, because of the amenities and location. They return because of the innkeepers.

Inns and B&Bs have become enormously popular, and some book rooms more than a year in advance. Whether you choose to make reservations online or by phone, do, always, make a reservation. Innkeepers will often ask when you plan to arrive, because they want to be there to greet you. If you're going to be late, please call to let them know your change of plans.

I happen to be a pick-up-the-phone-and-call traveler, and I recommend that method if you're going to a new lodging and you have questions or special requests. You can also ask about packages or special discounts that may not be on the inn's website. Here are some other things to consider when you talk to the innkeeper.

Bathrooms

Most inns these days have rooms with private baths. In fact, many of the bathrooms include luxurious tubs, plush robes and lovely toiletries. Some lodgings have rooms with private baths, as well as a couple of rooms that share a bath or share separate mens' and womens' baths. Sometimes the baths are private but not attached. And a private bath might include a tub and shower or just one or the other. If it matters, ask what comes with your room.

Beds

These days, I see mostly queen- and king-size beds, twins and kings that can become twins. Occasionally I find antique bedsteads that are double-bed-size or even three-quarter. If the size of the bed matters to you, ask what's available.

Rates

The prices quoted here range from lowest rate at low season to highest rate at high season, for double occupancy. A wide range of room prices often indicates that the inn has rooms with a variety of amenities. If you are quoted a rate that is more than you want to spend, ask if a less expensive room is available. If you're celebrating, consider asking about extras that the inn might offer such as flowers, massage or private dining.

The rates here are meant only to give you an idea of prices. For exact rates at the time you plan to travel, check the website or call the innkeeper.

Getting together

Many inns and B&Bs offer a happy hour or social hour before dinner. It's an absolutely charming tradition, and innkeepers say that guests frequently end up going out to dinner together. Such fun! If you can arrive in time to attend, do.

The annex?

At some inns, new additions have been built onto the original structure or are freestanding elsewhere on the grounds. If you have a preference as to wing, floor or building, let the innkeeper know when you make a reservation.

Eating well

Food options . . . wow! We are a delightful nation of gluten-free, dairy-free, sugar-free, egg-free, vegetarian and vegan diners, and most innkeepers have become skilled at meeting our needs—with some notice. If you have dietary preferences, let them know when you make a reservation, and remind them when you check in.

Children

If you plan to travel with children, do mention them when you make a reservation. Many innkeepers limit their rooms to a maximum of two people, and some inns are simply not appropriate—or fun—for youngsters. If an innkeeper tells you his or her lodging is not suitable for kids, believe it and go elsewhere. Inns that welcome children, however, often have toys, cribs, rollaways and plenty of space where kids can be . . . kids.

Our other kids

Pets permitted? Not usually, though some inns will accept a small pet in a designated pet-friendly room. Pets in residence? Several, often to the delight of guests. I've heard stories of guests sending sympathy cards when they learned that a dog or cat they had become fond of at an inn passed away. If you have allergies, phobias, or pet peeves, ask the innkeepers if their pets are permitted in quarters shared by guests.

Staying connected . . . or not

Most inns offer Wi-Fi now, so I usually only mention it when it might seem incongruent. For example, you won't see a car on Mackinac Island, but you can get your e-mail there! Many inns have cable or satellite TV. Some innkeepers have put TVs in common areas only, and others eschew them altogether. If you need to be connected, ask about availability before you make a reservation.

Settling up

Payment options vary greatly at inns. Some are not set up to process credit-card payments, although they will accept them to secure your reservation. If you plan to pay with anything other than cash, ask about your options.

Thump in the night

In the midst of signing copies of my first novel, *Spirits & Wine*, a mystery with a ghost in it, it occurred to me to ask innkeepers about otherworldly guests who might be walking their halls. I am delighted to say there are several, including one who is, I am quite certain, a cat!

With a little help from my friends

I'm deeply grateful to my friends Marcelaine Lewis and Steve Wilson, and to my husband, Paul Collins—a triumvirate who visited several inns and reported back with all the details I would have looked for. Marcelaine has lived on the Keweenaw Peninsula for decades and covered two inns there. Steve's family has had a home on Bois Blanc Island since 1973, and he contributed to the narrative on Insel Haus. Paul has hunted, fished and camped in both peninsulas since he was a teenager, and he met with several innkeepers as he made his way across the state over the past two years. He has also been my go-to guy, editor of my first drafts, and the best cheerleader I can imagine. The assistance of these three resulted in a better book, with fascinating background information and observations I likely would have missed.

I am also grateful to my friend Cathy Russell, owner of the White Swan Inn and past president of the Michigan Lake to Lake Bed and Breakfast Association. Cathy was a terrific sounding board as I gathered information for this edition, and she pointed me toward several innkeepers I otherwise might not have met.

In the mid-1980s, I was an enthusiastic but shy writer with a great idea for a book, a signed contract with this publisher, and a lot of innkeepers to talk with. It was a scary proposition that required me to call strangers to tell them about a book called *Michigan's Town and Country Inns* that would feature inns and bed-and-breakfast homes across the state, and to convince them I knew what I was doing.

Stafford Smith and his lovely Bay View Inn already had a national reputation for fine accommodations and food by the time I started researching that first edition of the book. The inn was one of the few in Michigan featured in national guidebooks at the time. Stafford was hugely respected in the industry, and he was, to me, larger than life. I was nervous when I met him, and he put me completely at ease. He was kind and generous. He offered complimentary lodging while I did research in the area, and over the years he has spent hours answering my questions and encouraging my efforts. Stafford taught me about the business of innkeeping by his gracious example, and I am very grateful to him.

I always intended this book to be, at its heart, a collection of stories. I want you to enjoy reading about these inns and learning about Michigan even if you never leave home, so I often ask innkeepers for anecdotes that I can share with you. Many are included here. They give an insider's look at this state's rich culture and history and a vision for its future that is being shaped, in part, by the innkeepers themselves. I am grateful to all of them for their openness, their generous offers of accommodations and their contagious love of people and innkeeping.

Sometimes things change. We update information as we get it, up to press time, but even as we put the final touches on this fifth edition, I can just about guarantee that somewhere an innkeeper is giving a prospective buyer a tour, and another is drawing up plans to add more rooms. Consider this book just a *taste* of all that Michigan has to offer in spectacular inns and bed-and-breakfast lodgings. Please use it as a springboard for your own tour of the state's back roads, blue roads and urban highways, and enjoy the adventure!

SUSAN NEWHOF
MAY 2013

NORTH COUNTRY:
THE UPPER PENINSULA

Ahmeek
Sand Hills Lighthouse Inn

Big Bay
Thunder Bay Inn

Blaney Park
Celibeth House Bed and Breakfast

Curtis
Chamberlin's Ole Forest Inn

Laurium
Laurium Manor Inn and Victorian Hall Bed and Breakfast

St. Ignace
The Boardwalk Inn

AHMEEK

Sand Hills Lighthouse Inn

When was the last time you slept in a lighthouse? Most old buildings have a certain mystique about them, and I find lighthouses particularly intriguing. To the sailors who navigate through raging storms, zero-visibility fog and deep darkness, lighthouses are like guardian angels, pointing the way to safe passage. In the days when lights were lit manually, the keepers of the lights took their work seriously. To let the light go out could spell disaster for a ship and its crew and passengers.

Sand Hills Lighthouse is the largest of its kind in the United States. Constructed in 1917 at the edge of Lake Superior, it was designed to house three lighthouse keepers and their families—a good plan given that residents of the lighthouse faced months of isolation during the long winters in Michigan's Upper Peninsula, or "UP." In 1939 the US Coast Guard took over Sand Hills and automated it, as it did over time with all the Great Lakes lighthouses. During World War II, the grounds served as a training site and hosted two hundred coastguardsmen. After the war, the lighthouse was vacated and remained unused for decades.

Bill Frabotta is intrigued by lighthouses, and he bought Sand Hills in 1961. He spent thirty summers there and used the property's Fog Signal station as his cottage. When he retired from a career as a portrait photographer downstate, he embarked on an ambitious renovation of the lighthouse, aided by friends and craftspeople, and opened for B&B guests in 1995.

You might expect from its rather austere, castlelike exterior that the interior would be similarly businesslike. But it's gorgeous Victorian from top to bottom, and the elegant furnishings complement original ornate crown moldings and the staircase balustrade. The walls are hung with paintings and some of Bill's own photographs. There are modern luxuries, too, such as air-conditioning and hydronic heat, which uses water as the source of warmth.

Each of the eight guest rooms has a king- or queen-size bed and private bathroom. Two rooms have whirlpool bathtubs and a balcony overlooking Lake Superior. Early morning risers can enjoy a spectacular sunrise from several perspectives—the rocky shore, the front porch and even the massive tower. In fact, the geography here is such that at some times of the year you can catch the sun both rising and setting over Lake Superior.

A full and fragrant breakfast is served at 9:30, and Bill's wife, Mary Mathews, says it has become legendary. It's served buffet style on top of an antique square grand piano in the dining room. Both Mary and Bill cook, and the food gets raves. No surprise there. Mary has won dozens of ribbons at county fairs for her baked goods. House specialties include her made-from-scratch sticky buns, Merry Mary sunshine soufflé and homemade English muffins. If you want to eat earlier or are departing early, Bill and Mary will be happy to provide you with juice, coffee and pastries. Let them know your plans when you check in.

Mary loves to play the piano, and she takes requests for just about anything from Chopin to Joplin. You're likely to hear her playing at any time of day and especially during breakfast and in the evening when she gives a short performance while guests partake of a sumptuous dessert.

Winters up here are a snow lover's paradise. Bring your cross-country skis if you want to head out across the 35 acres that surround the lighthouse and the groomed trails nearby. Summer days are long. The sun sets very late this far north, and you may be fortunate enough to see the spectacular light displays of aurora borealis over the lake. Within easy driving distance are museums and historic sites where you can explore the development of the mining industry on the Keweenaw Peninsula, and there are old copper mines you can tour. However you choose to spend your days in this unique region, save time for climbing the stairs to the top of the lighthouse tower where you can get a bird's-eye view of the rugged coastline here. It has changed little since the first keeper of the light scanned the horizon nearly one hundred years ago.

Vitals

rooms: 8 with private baths

pets permitted: no

pets in residence: none

open season: year-round

rates: $165 to $225

e-mail: sandhills@pasty.net

website: www.sandhillslighthouseinn.com

owners/innkeepers:
Mary Mathews and William Frabotta
Five Mile Point Road
PO Box 298
Ahmeek, MI 49901
906-337-1744

BIG BAY

Thunder Bay Inn

I went looking for inns with stories for this edition, and this one is likely to put you on the hunt for an old movie. Michigan Supreme Court justice John D. Voelker, whose pen name was Robert Traver, wrote a novel based on a 1952 murder case for which he was the defense attorney. The story caught the eye of all the right people in Hollywood, including director Otto Preminger, and in 1959 it was released under the same name as the book, *Anatomy of a Murder*. Sound familiar?

To make the film as authentic as possible, much of it was filmed in and around the town of Big Bay, where the actual murder took place, including the old warehouse turned hotel at the top of the hill.

This huge three-story structure was built in 1911 as a warehouse for the Brunswick Corporation, which used nearby timber to make wooden bowling pins. Henry Ford bought Brunswick in 1943 so he could use the timber for the wood trim on his cars. He also bought and renovated the warehouse, adding breeze-catching porches, a huge first-floor fireplace and big windows. Then he converted the second floor into rooms he used as an executive retreat. The whole place was sold after Ford died in 1947 and was eventually turned into a hotel.

When movie executives decided to use the building for their set, they added the shell of a large first-floor room, and they painted the whole place pink, which apparently showed up better than white in the black-and-white film. For several days, Big Bay residents rubbed elbows with the movie's stars, including Jimmy Stewart, George C. Scott, Lee Remick, Ben Gazzara, Eve Arden and Orson Bean, who stayed there.

Gretchen and Wayne Peacock bought this treasure in 2008. Gretchen was delighted to play a DVD of the movie for us and to point out items in the scenes ("See that water fountain on the wall?") that can still be seen in the hotel ("It's this one right here!").

The hotel was called Thunder Bay Inn in the movie, and the name

stuck. The big first-floor room built just for the set became the present dining room and bar. It's a favorite gathering spot for local residents, and it's there you'll be treated to some really good food orchestrated by the chef and general manager, Duke, the Peacock's talented son. The menu includes traditional pub fare plus locally caught whitefish, hearty south-of-the-border Mexican selections and a Wednesday all-you-can-eat spaghetti special that's made from Duke's grandmother's recipe. Duke is particularly proud of the prime rib he serves on Saturday night, and locals rave about the Friday fish fry.

There are twelve sleeping rooms on the second and third floors, and they have a variety of in-room sink, bathroom and shower options. Rooms with private baths are available, and guests staying in a room without a tub or shower may use one of the men's or women's shower rooms. Two rooms share a full bath, which is a great arrangement for families. The rooms are pretty and comfortable, and many of the furnishings are antique but not fussy. If you like, you can check out the photos on the website and choose your room in advance of your arrival. Each room has a ceiling fan, which is often all that's needed in summer in this far-north region. You can also request a room with a window air-conditioning unit. When you're ready to relax, make your way to a seat on the front porch where you get a fine view of little Lake Independence to the east.

If you visited the inn several years ago and haven't been back, you'll be delighted to see that the Peacocks tore up the old floor coverings in the massive foyer and living room and refinished the rich, buttery pine floorboards they found underneath. They add greatly to the welcoming feeling you'll get when you step inside. A buffet breakfast with fruit, cereals, hard-cooked eggs and breads is served there. And do take a look at the large display of newspaper clippings and photos from the inn's movie days.

We visited the Thunder Bay Inn in December, and I can attest to the fact that it's set up for winter comfort. It's a favorite base for cross-country skiers and snowmobilers, and you'll be snug whether you're curled up in front of the fireplace that Henry Ford added or warmed by the wood-burning stove in the dining room.

By the way, if you're interested in the spirits that still walk these old halls, ask the staff . . .

Vitals

rooms: 12. Some have private baths, some have a sink and toilet, and there are men's and women's shower rooms.

pets permitted: no

pets in residence: none

open season: year-round except April and closed around Thanksgiving and Christmas

rates: $70 to $120. Ask about group rates and a winter snowmobile "per-person" special.

e-mail: thunderbayinn@ironbay.net

website: www.ThunderBayInn.net

owners/innkeepers:
Wayne and Gretchen Peacock
400 Bensinger
PO Box 22
Big Bay, MI 49808
906-345-9220

BLANEY PARK

Celibeth House Bed and Breakfast

In 1985, the whole town of Blaney Park went up for auction. It wasn't a big town, but it did have a couple lodges, a few houses and storefronts, some small cabins and one fine mansion at the top of the hill. Wealthy lumber baron William Mueller had built the home for his family in 1895. The Earles, who owned the Wisconsin Land and Lumber Company, acquired it in 1911 and called it Celibeth—a combination of the names of two sisters, Cecilia and Elizabeth.

Nearby resident Elsa Strom had her eye on the mansion and inquired about its fate the day after the auction. Turns out it hadn't sold. She made an offer, got it, and opened it for bed-and-breakfast guests a couple of years later. The business was her passion, so when she thought about retiring, she called Roger and Darlene Cassady, who love history and participate in Revolutionary War reenactments. She thought they would be perfect as Celibeth's next innkeepers.

"Elsa asked if we would consider taking a look at this wonderful home and the B&B she had created there," remembers Darlene. "Roger and I walked into Celibeth, fell in love with it and two months later it was ours!"

Darlene used to own an antique shop, and she had fun handpicking antique furnishings for the home and putting family treasures to use. The china, for example, was her grandmother's. There are seven good-size, antique-filled sleeping rooms for guests, plus plenty of common areas where you can stretch out and settle in. The bright, enclosed front porch has a game table, and on chilly evenings, which are possible any time of the year in the UP, you'll likely find a fire crackling in the living room fireplace. The outside deck is a perfect place for morning coffee.

You'll find several choices in bed sizes—king, queen, doubles and twins, so if bed size matters to you, ask what's available. The Family Room has both a double bed and two twins, and it might be perfect if

you're traveling with children or friends. The second-floor Suite Room has an antique double bed and a private sitting room. All the sleeping rooms have private bathrooms.

Darlene loves to cook, and she serves a full breakfast each morning. In case you get hungry later in the day, dessert, coffee, tea and lemonade are always available. What you won't find here are televisions or computers, so come prepared to enjoy a good book, a quiet walk, croquet on the lawn, board and card games and the company of those you're traveling with. "This home was made for people," says Darlene. "I love it when it's full and you can hear their laughter!"

Blaney Park is about 90 minutes west of the Mackinac Bridge and just 1 mile north of U.S. 2, which runs across the southern edge of the Upper Peninsula. That puts you in a perfect location for taking day trips to all kinds of interesting places such as Pictured Rocks National Lakeshore, Hiawatha National Forest and the historic ghost town of Fayette. Then there's historic Blaney Park, itself, which Darlene and Roger describe as the "little historic village that refuses to quit living."

Vitals

rooms: 7 with private baths

pets permitted: no

pets in residence: none

open season: May to November 1

rates: $80 to $125

e-mail: none

website: www.celibethhousebnb.com

owners/innkeepers:
   Darlene and Roger Cassady
   4446N M-77 Highway
   Blaney Park, MI 49836-9106
   906-283-3409

CURTIS

Chamberlin's Ole Forest Inn

It was a blustery December night when Paul and I pulled up to Chamberlin's Ole Forest Inn. The driving had been difficult, even by Upper Peninsula standards. The temperature hovered around 32°F and the weather gods could not agree on rain or snow so we were getting both. Our finicky global positioning system (GPS) unit had quit altogether several hours earlier, and after logging 300 miles since lunch, we were tired.

Then . . . we opened our car doors and were greeted by the feels-like-home scent of a wood-burning fire and the promise of warmth and rest just inside. In 15 minutes, we were toasty, seated in comfy chairs a few feet from the inn's 10-foot-wide stone fireplace, crackling fire ablaze. We sipped wine and feasted on a sizable wedge of brie baked in pastry, puddled in a perfectly sweet-tart raspberry sauce and served with crackers and apple slices. And that was followed by a fragrant bowl of fresh mussels in garlic butter. Oh my!

This rock-solid, classic clapboard inn with its wide wraparound porch was built near the Curtis train station in the late 1800s to serve the needs of rail passengers. It was a popular place for years, but after the last passenger train ran from Grand Marais to Curtis on November 5, 1910, the lodging business dwindled quickly. After being closed for several years, the inn was purchased in 1924 by James Ostrander, who decided to move it to the edge of Big Manistique Lake, a half mile away. Trees were felled, limbs were removed, and the trunks were greased. Horses were hitched, and the building was rolled, literally, several feet each day to its present site. The process took three months. Ostrander renamed it the Forest Inn, and it operated until the 1970s.

Bud Chamberlin first saw the building in 1989 while snowmobiling in the area. And despite the fact that it had been closed for years and was in rough shape, he was smitten. He opened after a two-year renovation, and the inn has been a hub of hospitality in Curtis ever since.

There are several reasons to come here. For starters, the food is excellent. The fresh whitefish and prime rib are local favorites, and do try that amazing brie! There are two dining rooms on the first floor and a small, fully stocked bar. So if you can't spend the night, stop in for lunch or dinner. Enjoy your meal fireside, as we did, or take a seat on the veranda where you'll be treated to a spectacular view of the lake. Locals coming to eat often arrive by boat and tie up at the inn's ample dock.

If you're spending the night, you can choose from eleven lovely sleeping rooms in a variety of sizes on the second and third floors. Six have private baths. We stayed in an elegant corner room that has French doors opening to a huge bathroom with a jetted tub and separate shower. The large Chamberlain Suite on the third floor has a marvelous view of the lake and a sitting area with a futon couch. Three rooms facing the lake each have a queen-size bed and a sink in the room, and they share two bathrooms—one for men and one for women. Two rooms with private baths have two double beds apiece, and two others share one adjoining bath—all great options if you're traveling with children or friends. You'll find pretty antiques and lots of attention to detail in the sleeping rooms, and even the smallest offers plenty of space for two guests. A hearty breakfast is served in the dining room or out on the veranda—your choice.

Kelly, Bud's wife, is a skilled florist and decorator, and her talents are evident everywhere. During our visit, the inn was bedecked for Christmas with festive boughs and branches, tiny white lights, candles and poinsettias and a gorgeous fresh tree.

Bud and Kelly love music, and they host an array of talented musicians and musical events throughout the year. Both are also active volunteers with Curtis's Erickson Center for the Arts, just a few miles from the inn, where you can take art classes and attend concerts and theater productions. Big Manistique Lake has good fishing, and the area is a paradise for snowmobilers. It's a mile across the water from the inn to the lake's tiny island—a good destination for kayakers—and the inn has kayaks you may use. The kitchen staff will be happy to pack you a lunch to go. A deck off the second floor has a hot tub for guests' use—a great pleasure after a day of playing in the snow! And for some extra pampering, you can arrange for a private massage. If you're looking for a spot to propose, I recommend the gazebo at the edge of the bluff.

This inn is a treasure, and it would be pure pleasure to spend several days here and never leave the area. However, if you plan to wander the UP a bit, it's an easy drive from Curtis to places such as the Seney Wildlife Refuge, Pictured Rocks and Tahquamenon Falls.

Vitals

rooms: 11, 6 have private baths, 3 share 2 baths and 2 share an adjoining bath.

pets permitted: no

pets in residence: none

open season: year-round except April

rates: $89 to $130

e-mail: info@chamberlinsinn.com

website: www.chamberlinsinn.com

owners/innkeepers:
Kelly and Bud Chamberlin
P.O Box 307
N9450 Manistique Lakes Road
Curtis, MI 49820
906-586-6000
800-292-0440

LAURIUM

Laurium Manor Inn and Victorian Hall Bed and Breakfast

Laurium Manor and Victorian Hall are two breathtaking mansions that stand as tributes to the wealth that was generated by Upper Peninsula copper mines in the late nineteenth and early twentieth centuries.

Located in the heart of the Keweenaw Peninsula, the 13,000-square-foot Laurium Manor was completed in 1908 for Thomas H. Hoatson Jr., who owned the Calumet and Arizona Mining Company. He spent $50,000 on the construction of the home, which he lovingly built as a surprise for his wife and children. Then he spent another $35,000 to furnish its forty-five rooms. Yes, forty-five rooms! To put the cost in perspective, miners at the time were making twenty-five cents an hour. Laurium Manor, you see, was not destined to be an ordinary mansion.

Innkeeper Julie Sprenger, a native of Iron Mountain, never forgot her first look at the Manor when she was a child. When she met future husband Dave at Michigan Technological University, she took him to see it, and he was captivated as well. After graduating from college, the Sprengers moved to California but soon longed to return to the Upper Peninsula. Their opportunity to purchase the Manor came in 1989, and they decided that this legacy to mining had to be shared.

Remarkably, much of the home's opulence, including gilded-leather wall coverings, silver-leaf ceilings, stained glass, marble, artisan-quality hand-carved woodwork and expansive verandas, had survived the decades mostly intact. As you might expect, the rooms are huge. The reception hall alone is 12 by 40 feet, and the ballroom is 50 by 50 feet. Some of the sleeping rooms are more than 500 square feet. The Laurium Suite, for example, is 630 square feet and has both a king-size, eight-foot-tall cherry and ash canopy bed with marble columns and an original Hoatson family, dark mahogany double bed. It also has a gas-log

fireplace and a huge private balcony. Julie and Dave have been told that Theodore Roosevelt stayed in this room during his campaign here for president in 1912.

After much research, the Sprengers completed their masterful restoration and opened the home for bed-and-breakfast guests.

A few years later, the owners of Victorian Hall, just across the street, suggested to Dave and Julie that they buy it as well. Though taking on a second mansion would be daunting for most of us, they jumped at the suggestion and opened it for guests two days after they took possession of it.

Victorian Hall is somewhat smaller—just 7,500 square feet, which, by ordinary mansion standards, is still big! And its soaring ceilings make it seem even larger. Among its surviving comforts are six carved fireplaces, four of which are in sleeping rooms. As in the Manor, the extravagant architectural fashions of the day—stained glass, ornate woodwork and decorative plasterwork—can be seen everywhere.

Antiques and wicker fill both inns, so appropriate for the period when these homes were built, and the dramatic wall colors, fine carpets and artwork, fabrics and window treatments that Julie and Dave added complement the homes' original features. Hoatson's sweet tribute to his Scottish heritage is still evident in the thistle design on the face of a fireplace inlaid with stained glass and gold leaf. The grand three-story staircase in the Manor, crafted from hand-carved oak, is as magnificent as when it was new. My friend Marcelaine says she stood at the foot of it and could hear the happy laughter of children—the Hoatson children and their friends, perhaps—echoing around it.

While the Manor has an art nouveau flavor, Victoria Hall is pure Victorian. In the midst of all this historic elegance and restored detail, the Sprengers have added up-to-date technology for their guests, including wireless Internet.

Guests of both inns are invited to a breakfast buffet at the Manor, served between 8:00 and 10:00 a.m. When I called the Manor on a cool June morning and asked what was for breakfast, Julie said she was serving a pear and rosemary upside-down coffee cake, build-your-own parfaits with fruit and granola, and orzo and eggs with fresh lemon, parmesan cheese and fresh basil. Oh my! The buffet usually includes a breakfast meat as well, plus their newest addition: French bread with homemade flavored peanut butters. Their pomegranate peanut butter is a huge success, and so is the cinnamon-current. Julie says she tries out new recipes on the neighbors. Those are some lucky neighbors!

When you first walk into either inn, you may feel as though you just entered a museum. In fact, when the inns are open, Julie offers daytime tours. But these are not museums. The inns have been restored with guests' comfort in mind, and you are invited to explore them. Staying

here offers you the rare opportunity to take your time and experience firsthand the kind of luxury that flourished when copper reigned. Julie and Dave hope you'll feel relaxed and well cared for and that you'll enjoy living like a copper baron for a while.

If you know anything at all about the Upper Peninsula, you likely know that this is big snow country. Skiers and snowmobilers love it! But there is more to the Keweenaw than snow. Festivals and productions at the Calumet Theater provide great entertainment, and you're never far from antique shops and historic museums where you can learn all about this area's mining history. There are even a few ghost towns to explore.

If you're looking for accommodations for several people traveling together and you plan to be based in Laurium for several days, ask Dave and Julie about their vintage vacation rental homes just a block from the inns. Each has a complete kitchen, living room and dining room plus pretty bedrooms and bathrooms—plenty of space to settle in and call home while you explore the region. You'll find details on Laurium Manor's website.

Vitals

rooms: 10 in Laurium Manor, 8 in Victorian Hall, all with private baths

pets permitted: no

pets in residence: 2 cats for one week in April and one week in October, which stay primarily in the innkeepers' quarters

open season: usually May through October, plus four weeks around the Winter Carnival in January and February

rates: $89 to $175

e-mail: info@laurium.info

website: www.laurium.info

owners/innkeepers:
Julie and Dave Sprenger
320 Tamarack Street
Laurium, MI 49913
906-377-2549

ST. IGNACE

The Boardwalk Inn

Small city hotels have always had an appeal, so I was delighted to discover The Boardwalk Inn. I use the word *discover* loosely because hundreds of other travelers have known about it for decades! The hotel was built with two stories in 1928, in the heart of downtown St. Ignace, right across the street from Lake Huron. Lodging rooms were on the second floor, and the first floor was a lobby and restaurant. It was called the Travelers Inn.

In the 1930s, the restaurant was moved out of the hotel, and the space it had occupied was converted to several small sleeping rooms. A third floor was added in the late 1950s or early 1960s. But, as was the fate of so many small-town hotels, it eventually fell into disrepair.

Jim Krug, a native of Bad Axe, Michigan, moved to Texas when he was eighteen and met and fell in love with a charming Texan named Kayla. They married and lived in several places, but nothing felt like home. So they turned their eyes to Michigan, and Jim, who had always wanted to own a hotel, went online to see what might be available.

"He called me to come look at a listing," recalls Kayla, who dreamed of buying an old house and restoring it, "and I fell in love with the website!" Luckily for the Krugs, the sellers had purchased the hotel years earlier, when it was in near ruins, did a huge renovation and developed a successful bed-and-breakfast business.

"We bought it turnkey," says Kayla. "We brought a few pieces of our own and moved in with reservations on the book!" And, though she and Jim had few concerns about this big change in their lives, Kayla admits to sitting in the parking lot when they arrived, looking up at the three-story hotel they had just purchased and thinking, "What did we get ourselves into?"

That was in 2002, and what they got themselves into has been great. The guests have been wonderful, Kayla says. Many come back year after

year for events in the area, and some have become their friends. One couple stayed there on their honeymoon, and they return every year, now with their son. Another couple came back with their children and grandchildren. "Three generations!," says Kayla. "We've become a part of some family traditions."

Guests who come to town to attend the annual car show return to the inn every year, and so do enthusiasts of the annual Richard Crane Truck Show. "It's like a minireunion when they all get here!," laughs Kayla.

When you walk into the huge lobby, you'll likely notice the 14-foot ceilings, beautiful woodwork and stately open stairway to the second floor. You'll see an old switchboard, too, which once belonged to the

phone company. When it was no longer being used, Jim asked if he might have it. His mother was the chief operator in Bad Axe, and he liked the connection. There are also registration books going back to the hotel's earliest days. If you're feeling like a game of checkers, you'll find a table and chairs in the window with a checkerboard waiting.

Oh . . . and there's a 1967 Harley-Davidson motorcycle. In the lobby. Jim can tell you the story.

There are four guest rooms on the first floor and eight more on the third floor. Most are very large, with room to settle in for a few days, owing to the fact that most are two original rooms combined to make one. There are also two suites, each of which has two bedrooms and two baths. All the rooms are pretty and comfy with lots of country touches and antiques. All the beds are queen size, and some of the quilts on them were made by Kayla. Some of the third-floor rooms have great views of the bay or Mackinac Island. Each room has air-conditioning and a private bath. Rooms on the first floor have tub-shower combos. Third-floor rooms have showers.

On the second floor, you'll find the Fireside Room, where breakfast is served, and where guests often gather to play games or cards. It has a cozy gas-log hearth that blazes on chilly days. Kayla and Jim have living quarters on the second floor, too, which means one of them is almost always close by in case you need something.

For early risers, coffee is ready at 6:30 a.m. A breakfast buffet with bagels and English muffins, oatmeal and cold cereals, juice and hot beverages is set up at 8:00 a.m.

The inn is across the street from a beautiful pedestrian boardwalk that follows the Lake Huron shoreline. Shops and restaurants are nearby. The boat docks for the three companies that ferry people to Mackinac Island are within walking distance. "Quite a few of our guests come in for the night and leave early in the morning to spend the day on the island," says Kayla. "Then they come back in the evening to spend a second night with us."

Vitals

rooms: 12 rooms with private baths, including 2 suites with 2 bedrooms and 2 baths

pets permitted: no

pets in residence: none

open season: May through the third week in October

rates: $65 to $150

e-mail: bwih@sbcglobal.net

website: www.boardwalkinn.com

owners/innkeepers:
Kayla and Jim Krug
316 North State Street
St. Ignace, MI 49781
906-643-7500
800-254-5408

ISLANDS IN THE STRAITS: BOIS BLANC ISLAND AND MACKINAC ISLAND

Bois Blanc Island
Insel Haus

Mackinac Island
Cloghaun
Metivier Inn

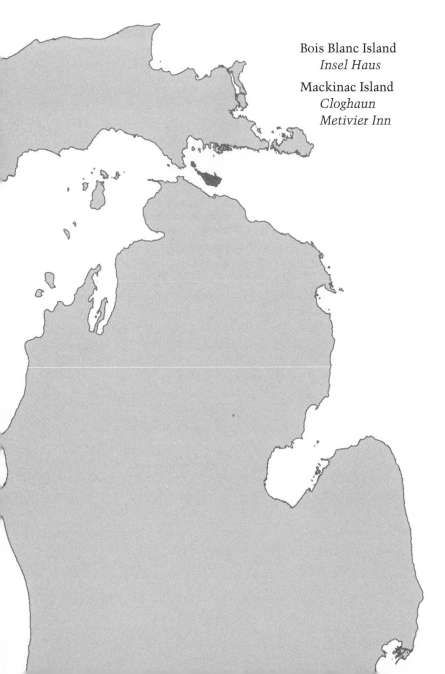

Getting there
By Steve Wilson

To solve the decades-long problem of crossing the Straits of Mackinac, Horatio Earle, Michigan's first highway commissioner, proposed connecting the Lower and Upper Peninsulas with a series of floating bridges linking Bois Blanc Island, Round Island and Mackinac Island. While that would have made travel between the islands easy, it would have been a laborious process to get from one peninsula to the other, and would have brought unwelcome traffic to the otherwise peaceful islands. After decades of planning and three and a half years of construction, the 5-mile-long Mackinac Bridge between Mackinaw City and St. Ignace opened on November 1, 1957.

Kurt Plaunt was studying for the US Coast Guard exam to gain his captain's license when I first met him forty years ago. At the time, his father was captain of the ferry that transported us to Bois Blanc along the route first licensed by Kurt's grandfather. Today Kurt's son and nephew work beside him as fourth-generation captains on the *Kristen D*, a fifteen-car ferry that makes the trip between the island and Cheboygan eight times daily during the summer.

[Note: Many thanks to Steve Wilson, whose family has had a home on Bois Blanc Island since 1973 and who contributed this sidebar and a good deal of the Insel House narrative.]

BOIS BLANC ISLAND

Insel Haus

If once you have slept on an island
You'll never be quite the same

Poet Rachel Lyman Field (1894–1942) could have been sitting by a fireside window at Insel Haus bed and breakfast when she penned those
lines above. The inn is just a short drive from the ferry dock on Bois
Blanc Island, located in Michigan's Straits of Mackinac, and the lure
of the island is as real as the water that surrounds it. Just ask Christa
Newhouse.

"I fell in love with the flaming red and orange colors of the maple
trees in the yard, surrounded by the deep green cedars and hemlocks,"
she remembers of her first look at this former hunting lodge. It is one of
the island's largest homes, and a few of its owners have added to its sto-
ried past, including the Fisher family, whose distinctive Body by Fisher
trademark graced every General Motors car until the 1980s.

Christa purchased the lodge from Pete Fisher in 1980. Then she literally "raised the roof," reengineering the sprawling gable-fronted home
to make it suitable as an inn, a retreat center and a year-round residence for her and her husband Shelby. Together they strive to create an
environment in sync with nature and the island. They'll fill your stay
with splendid stories of an island culture on this adventurous and often
overlooked gem among the Great Lakes State's 350 islands. They also
have fascinating stories of Christa's youth in Berlin during the years following World War II and of the couple's Emmy Award–winning career
in commercial filmmaking.

Insel Haus, "island house" in German, Christa's native language, is
filled with European and American antiques, Persian rugs, stained glass
windows and abundant rich woodwork. Perhaps as a memento of the
island's central location in eighteenth- and nineteenth-century shipping

channels, a large wooden ship's wheel converted to a chandelier hangs before a massive stone fireplace. The shores of Lake Huron, at times sandy and at times stony, provide picturesque views from many of the rooms.

There are nine sleeping rooms here, plus nine bathrooms, three kitchens, three laundry rooms and four common rooms. The floor plan is such that accommodations can be configured just about any way you need them, from a single room with a shared bath and laundry to a luxurious suite, or multiple sleeping rooms with private baths, fireplaces, a porch or deck, a kitchen and a great room. The inn's website includes photos of each room plus a floor plan to show you the locations of the rooms and their possible combinations. It's amazingly flexible and pretty ingenious!

Accommodations include a sumptuous buffet breakfast, which usually includes breads and jams, baked goods from Christa's favorite bakery in Traverse City, different kinds of sausages and cheeses (including Brie), fruit and juice, yogurt and cereal, plus a hot dish such as quiche or Christa's special German-style apple pancakes.

"People love Bois Blanc," Christa says, adding that some of her returning guests count themselves among the island's nearly two thousand summer residents. Only about seventy hearty souls live here all year. Shelby, who had never been north of Bay City, Michigan, before moving to Bois Blanc, recommends a winter stay at Insel Haus for a truly memorable addition to anyone's bucket list.

Christa is a fiber artist and knitwear designer, and she creates stunning clothing and art. She often leads gatherings of knitters in the large retreat center located behind the house, which can accommodate up to twenty-two people and is a favorite site for business meetings, workshops, weddings and other special events.

Exploring Bois Blanc Island is as adventurous as you choose to make it. Locals have organized a sightseeing map featuring more than a dozen sites, including a one-room schoolhouse still in use, a lighthouse and a Coast Guard chapel. If you're a little more daring, try mountain biking, hiking, kayaking or sport fishing. The gravel roads are easy to navigate and provide spectacular views of the Mackinac Bridge, which spans Michigan's two peninsulas, and woodland settings filled with deer.

The most common way to arrive on the island is by ferry from Cheboygan. When you step aboard, says Christa, "you leave the rest of the world behind." The 35-minute ride will take you past the US Coast Guard icebreaker *Mackinac,* a wetland nesting ground for swans and the Mackinac Bridge, affectionately referred to here as the Mighty Mac. Plaunt Transportation will ferry you and your car to the island from downtown Cheboygan from May 1 through November 30. A local air service in St. Ignace offers flights to the island. If you choose not to bring your car, Shelby will pick you up at the dock.

Vitals

> *rooms:* 9 that can be combined and configured to include private and shared baths, kitchens, sitting rooms, decks and other features
>
> *pets permitted:* yes, well-behaved dogs by special arrangement
>
> *pets in residence:* none
>
> *open season:* year-round
>
> *rates:* $105 to $185
>
> *e-mail:* christa@inselhausbandb.com
>
> *website:* http://www.inselhausbandb.com
>
> *owners/innkeepers:*
> Christa and Shelby Newhouse
> HCR 1, Box 157
> Bois Blanc Island, MI 49775
> 248-921-2890
> 888-634-7393

Mackinac Island

Magic is how visitors often describe Mackinac Island, and the word fits. What else can you say about an island where motor vehicles have been prohibited since 1898 and bicycles and horse-drawn carriages are the primary modes of transportation? This is a land where a population of 4,000 summer residents drops to 450 hardy souls after Halloween and the 650,000 tourists who fill the streets between May and October disappear. When ice forms a bridge to the mainland in deep winter, the ice road is marked with postholiday Christmas trees.
Magic!

Mackinac Island occupies just under 4 square miles at the north end of Lake Huron—a location so strategic that the British built forts there during the Revolutionary War. It was the scene of two battles during the War of 1812.

By the end of the nineteenth century, the island had become a popular tourist attraction and a summer residence for wealthy families. Grand cottages lined the bluffs. Horses and bicycles provided transportation. Much of the island has undergone extensive historical preservation since then, and the entire island has been designated as a National Historic Landmark. More than 80 percent of the island is Mackinac Island State Park.

So . . . imagine waking to the gentle clip-clop of horses and the squeak of buggy wheels, the cooling lake breezes that have lured those seeking relief from summer heat for 150 years, the promise of a picturesque bicycle ride and a walk through a butterfly conservatory. Consider parasailing for a bird's-eye view or take a trail ride. Buy fudge! It may be the island's official food, and some of the confectionaries have been making it there for more than 100 years. Walk through Fort Mackinac, built in 1780. Breathe history.

Hotels, guest houses, inns and B&Bs are located throughout the busy downtown area and beyond, offering stories that go back to its earliest European settlers and plenty of island hospitality. Cloghaun and Metivier are longtime favorites.

Mackinac Island can be reached by private boat, by ferry from St. Ignace and Mackinaw City, by small aircraft, and in the winter by snowmobile over that tree-lined ice road. The airport has a 3,500-foot paved runway, and there is charter air service from the mainland. As for that 1898 ruling about cars . . . few exceptions have been made. Emergency and service vehicles may be used when necessary, and snowmobiles provide winter transportation. Contact the Mackinac Island Tourism Bureau for more information.

MACKINAC ISLAND

Cloghaun

In 1848, the year of the great famine in Ireland, Thomas and Bridget Donnelley left their beloved little Irish town of Cloghaun and set out for Mackinac Island. They had a relative on the island, Charles O'Malley, who was a prosperous trader and the owner of a hotel called the Island House. The decision to move there must have seemed right. Thomas and Bridget began to put down roots. Four years after arriving, they bought land near the business district, and in 1884 they built a fine home there to house their large family. They later turned it into a tourist home and named it Cloghaun, which is Gaelic, meaning "land of little stones." Cloghaun and descendants of the Donnelleys have been welcoming travelers ever since.

James Bond is the great-grandson of Thomas and Bridget. His mother was their granddaughter. He has spent summers on the island since he was a baby, and his mother ran Cloghaun until she died in 1990. "She was a pack rat and saved everything!," says James. And lucky for him, that meant that all the old deeds, papers and photos pertaining to the house were never thrown away. Oh, and there were one hundred years' worth of furnishings as well.

James embarked on an ambitious renovation of Cloghaun to convert it from a tourist home into an elegant, history-filled bed and breakfast. He took off part of the back of the house, which was deteriorating, and replaced it with a 15-foot addition, and he restored the front porches, using old photos for reference. All the rooms got a facelift, and all but two of the sleeping rooms got private baths.

James also opened up the original dining room, which had been closed for seventy-five years, and what treasures he found! "It was filled with great furniture," he recalls, "all the original pieces, and in excellent condition, because no one had touched them for so long."

The eleven guest rooms are furnished with many of those original

pieces—ornate Victorian bedsteads, marble-topped tables and dressers—plus antiques that James has gathered over the years. The rooms are named for family members. Two have balconies and one has a private entrance.

I especially love the four-poster, lace-topped canopy beds in Nellie's Room and Bridget's Room. Anna's Room is very large and has two double beds. Take a little time to look at the documents on the walls. You'll find treasures such as a marriage certificate and pension papers that help tell the story of the Donnelley family and their descendants.

What you won't find in the rooms are TVs or air-conditioners. "We're keeping the home as true to the original as possible," says James, "And guests tell us they love it."

If you arrive at the inn between 3:00 and 5:00 p.m., you'll be there in time to enjoy tea and baked goods. Tea is a lovely tradition here, and I recommend you take it to the porch where you can relax and people watch. The inn sits one block back from the main street and harbor, and it is several steps above street level, so it offers a peaceful respite from the seasonal bustle of tourists coming and going, yet it's close to everything. From that wonderful porch, you get a grand view of Cloghaun's lush front gardens, and you can see all the way to the harbor.

When you're done exploring the island for the day and you've bought all the fudge you'll need for the next year, you can settle back in the home's large library for a little rest. It's stocked with both contemporary books and volumes that have been passed down through the family. It also has a fireplace, a VCR and movies.

A breakfast buffet is available from 8:00 to 10:00 a.m. It includes a hot entrée, homemade baked goods, fruits and beverages. In good weather, guests love to eat on the porch where they can watch the island begin to stir. Since cars are not permitted on the island, the street "traffic" is people on foot, bicycles and horse-drawn carriages! In spite of it looking like the 1800s outside your door, Cloghaun has wireless Internet, in case you need to stay connected.

When I talked recently to innkeeper Paul Carey, I asked if Halloween is still a big deal on the island. He says it is, and he should know. He and his mother have been innkeepers at Cloghaun since 1997. Paul says everyone who hasn't migrated back to the mainland by the end of October dresses in costume, and there are parties everywhere. Sounds like a great way to close out the season on this fairy-tale island.

Vitals

rooms: 11, all but 2 with private baths

pets permitted: no

pets in residence: 1 beloved springer spaniel named Maggie, who is not allowed in the guests' areas

open season: May through Halloween

rates: $80 to $195

e-mail: cloghaun@aol.com

website: www.cloghaun.com

owner: James Bond

innkeepers:
Marti and Paul Carey, mother and son
PO Box 1540
Mackinac Island, MI 49757
906-847-3885
888-442-5929

MACKINAC ISLAND

Metivier Inn

The Metivier family has a fascinating history, which the present owners of the Metivier Inn have documented back to 1700, when Jean François Metivier immigrated to the newly formed French province of Quebec. One of his descendants, Louis Metivier, was a Civil War veteran when he and his wife, Josephine Lambert, purchased an old French cabin in 1877 next to the oldest house on Mackinac Island. Within a few years, they built a new home there for their growing family of seven children.

Louis died at the age of sixty-one in 1902, leaving Josephine with three children under the age of sixteen. She moved into the home's summer kitchen at the back of the house and rented out the front to make ends meet. Her unmarried daughter, Mary Sophia, inherited the house in return for having cared for her. When Mary Sophia died in 1959, it went to her youngest sister, Mabel, and was later passed to Mabel's children.

Michael Bacon had summered on Mackinac Island as a child, and he loved it there. When he completed medical school, he began providing relief coverage for the local doctor and eventually became the island clinic's medical director. He was delighted to be able to purchase the Metivier home when it came up for sale; amazingly, it was still owned by a member of the Metivier family.

In 1983, Michael and his wife, Jane, joined forces with Jane's brother, Ken Neyer, and his wife, Diane, and began transforming the nineteenth-century home into the lovely, luxurious inn you see today. They renovated it from top to bottom, adding a new east wing, a distinctive turret and a spacious veranda that extends the length of the inn. Over the years, two more additions and another turret were skillfully completed. The inn now has twenty-two guest rooms, and it is impossible to tell where the original home ends and the new begins.

Drawing from the influences that have dominated the island at vari-

ous times, Metivier is decorated with country French and English furnishings, floral wall coverings, classic bedsteads, including four-posters and canopies, crisp cotton fabrics and sophisticated touches that make each room feel quite special. One of the most popular is the romantic Jacuzzi Room with its pretty country French style and both a Jacuzzi tub and a private deck. The John Jacob Astor Room has a summery cottage feel and a fine four-poster bed plus a sitting area in one of the turrets. Some rooms have two beds or a pull-out sofa and can accommodate four guests. All the rooms are individually air-conditioned and have flat-screen TVs and Wi-Fi.

A hot buffet breakfast is served in the spacious first-floor lobby from 7:30 to 9:30 a.m. You'll find a variety of choices, including breads and pastries, an egg casserole, yogurts, hard-boiled eggs, oatmeal, dry cereals and fruit. Sometimes you'll be treated to house specialties such as bread pudding and cobblers. Blueberries and other local fruits are served in season. There's plenty to satisfy everyone's taste. There are warm pine tables for inside dining, plus a cozy fireplace that's ablaze when the weather turns chilly. You're also welcome to have breakfast on the veranda so you can watch the island wake up. In the tradition of English teatime, beverages and sweets—and sometimes island-made fudge—are set out for guests at 3:00 p.m.

I love many things about this gracious inn, and one of them is the location. Metivier faces Market Street, one block back from the island's busy main street, perfect for getting away—but not too far away—from the daytime hustle and bustle.

I also love the gardens. Diane has a way with flowers, and against a backdrop of the inn's white picket fences and arbor, her French country gardens are a vision of vintage charm. Don't be surprised to see people stopping to take photographs of them. It happens all the time. They are that beautiful. From the backyard of the inn, there's a great view of the Grand Hotel and its golf course, which borders the inn, and the Governor's Mansion up the hill. There's a tranquil sitting area there, too, and more of Diane's gardens and Adirondack chairs for relaxing. Across the street from the inn are stables for some of the island's many horses. When you stay at Metivier, you have easy access to the restaurants, shops, boat docks and museums so you can move easily between the touristy fun stuff on the island and the peacefulness of this historic home turned inn.

Vitals

rooms: 22 with private baths

pets permitted: no

pets in residence: none

open season: mid-May to the end of October

rates: $120 to $320

e-mail: info@metivierinn.com

website: www.metivierinn.com

owners: Jane and Michael Bacon, Diane and Ken Neyer

innkeepers:
David and Blanca Prentler
PO Box 285
Mackinac Island, MI 49757
866-847-6234

LAND OF LITTLE BAYS:
NORTHERN LOWER PENINSULA

Bay View
The Terrace Inn

Bellaire
Bellaire Bed and Breakfast
The Grand Victorian Bed and
Breakfast Inn

Charlevoix
Horton Creek Inn Bed
and Breakfast

Leland
The Riverside Inn

Ludington
Ludington House Bed and Breakfast
Cartier Mansion

Old Mission Peninsula
Chateau Chantal Winery and Inn
The Inn at Chateau Grand Traverse

Pentwater
Hexagon House

Petoskey
Stafford's Bay View Inn

Prudenville
Springbrook Inn

Suttons Bay
The Inn at Black Star Farms

Traverse City
Antiquities Wellington Inn

Walloon Lake Village
Walloon Lake Inn

Wolverine
Silent Sport Lodge Wilderness Bed and Breakfast

BAY VIEW

The Terrace Inn

Perhaps, like a good parent, I should not have favorites, but I do. Some inns stood out twenty-five years ago when I wrote the first edition of this book . . . and they still do. The Terrace Inn is one of them. Tucked up in the hills of Bay View, the inn has been hosting guests for more than one hundred years, and it just keeps getting better. Each successive renovation has made it prettier and more comfortable, and I've always loved the lobby fireplace . . . but I'm getting ahead of myself.

The Bay View Association was established in 1875 by the Methodist Church on a 430-acre plot of land overlooking Little Traverse Bay. It was part of the Chautauqua movement, which provided facilities for intellectual and scientific study and music and the arts, emphasizing religion and morality. Hundreds of Victorian-style summer homes were built on the acreage in the late nineteenth and early twentieth centuries, and land was set aside for commercial lodging, which is how The Terrace Inn came to be.

In its early years, the inn was a popular destination for the overflow of guests at nearby cottages. Accommodations were simple, and meals were served in the elegant hemlock-paneled dining room. In keeping with the rules of Bay View, the inn and all the homes were opened in the spring and closed in the fall.

Renovations through the years have paid tribute to the inn's historic roots while being mindful of the tastes and expectations of travelers today. The furnishings are lovely. Each of the thirty-seven guest rooms is decorated individually, and some of the smaller rooms have been combined to make larger rooms and spacious suites. Fireplaces and whirlpool tubs have been added to several, and most have window air-conditioners. Guest rooms on the second and third floors are reached by means of a stately open staircase. The large guest rooms on the first floor are good choices if you find stairs daunting.

One big change made in the last couple of decades is that The Ter-

Ghost hunting

If you're interested in a little paranormal search in the off-season, check The Terrace Inn's schedule of ghost-hunting adventures. Patty says that paranormal activity, recorded as electronic voice phenomena (EVP), has been captured at the inn.

Abby Sweet—yes, the name of the tea shop—is the name that was deciphered via EVP. After a year of research, investigators identified her as a maid who is known to have arrived at the inn but whose family never heard from her again.

race Inn is now open year-round. I have stayed there within a week of both the winter and summer solstices and found them equally wonderful times to visit. Let me tell you, first, about winter in Bay View, because it is magical, and it's something early guests did not get to experience. Except for the inn, the Bay View neighborhood is officially closed from fall to spring, and the road that runs past the inn is the only one plowed. That leaves its web of hilly streets snow-covered and perfect for snowshoeing and gentle cross-country skiing. It's peaceful and quiet, and when the nighttime sky is clear, the stars are big and bright.

On Saturday nights in January and February, when the weather is right, you can reserve a ride on a horse-drawn sleigh that picks up guests at the inn. Follow that with a couple hours sitting in front of the cozy lobby fireplace with a good novel and you have, in my mind, a perfect evening. If you're looking for a quiet winter getaway, The Terrace Inn is a great choice. In fact, you may find yourself hoping for a blizzard that will keep you snowed in here for days.

A visit in the summer is equally enchanting. Bay View becomes a busy place, and there are lots of outdoor activities in which you can take part, including tennis, hiking and swimming in the bay. The Bay View Association still offers a wonderful summer program of music, worship, lectures and seminars within walking distance and open to the public. And then there's that marvelous terrace, for which the inn is named. It's a fine place to rest with a cup of coffee or an ice cream cone. Do take time to look at the art there, too. Innkeepers Mo and Patty Rave host a different artist at the inn each week during the summer and display their creations.

An ample breakfast buffet is included with your lodging all year. During the summer months, the dining room is open daily for dinner for both guests and the public. In the off-season, it's open on weekends. The menu emphasizes ingredients that are fresh and local. The beef is grass

fed, herbs come from the inn's garden, and the planked whitefish is, as it has been for years, a favorite of local residents and returning guests. For a delightful summer afternoon treat, stop by Abby's Sweet Shop and Tea Room in the lower level of the inn for brewed tea, scones and tea sandwiches, Devonshire cream, jam and lemon curd.

Vitals

rooms: 37 on three stories, all with private baths

pets permitted: no

pets in residence: none

open season: year-round

rates: $99 to $179

e-mail: info@theterraceinn.com

website: www.theterraceinn.com

owners/innkeepers:
Mo and Patty Rave
1549 Glendale
PO Box 266
Bay View, MI 49770
800-530-9898

BELLAIRE

Bellaire Bed and Breakfast

David Schulz and Jim Walker owned a big home in the historic district of Ionia, Michigan, and after friends enjoyed their creative cooking and spent the night, they often remarked, "You two should open a B&B!"

So they did.

When I ask, "Why Bellaire?," Jim smiles and says simply, "Take a look around."

It is my first trip to this quiet village, nestled in the middle of the Chain of Lakes, anchored by Torch Lake, and it takes only a brief drive through the neighborhoods and surrounding countryside to understand its enormous appeal. The clear lakes and wooded hillsides, quaint stores and small-town friendliness, plus a host of year-round world-class recreational options have a lot to offer both residents and vacationers. But you don't have to leave the inn to love it here. The saying goes, "You had me at . . ." Well, Bellaire had *me* at the long driveway lined with sugar maples, the lush landscape and the broad lawn that rises gently up to the inn, the wide wraparound porches and giant pillars. Oh, yes . . . and the plate of perfectly rich iced cherry scones pressed into my hands when I left, which I intended to bring home but devoured before I reached the county line.

The original home here was built in 1879 by Emily and Richard Nixon. Emily was the niece of Henry Richardi who built the Grand Victorian Inn, just a block away. Richard made his fortune from the dry goods store and grocery he owned in Bellaire. He and Emily raised produce for the store in gardens on the property and had orchards and vineyards on their land as well. Emily lived to be nearly a hundred and remained in this home until the 1950s.

David and Jim bought the Nixon home in 1997. From its many rooms, they created five luxurious guest accommodations, plus a library paneled in native cherry with a stunning coffered ceiling and a fireplace.

Bellaire

The woods and water of this scenic area have attracted people for centuries. Europeans came in the nineteenth century when lumber was in great demand, and numerous waterways gave manufacturers a way to ship products from this region to the rest of the country. By the early twentieth century, Bellaire had an assortment of grocery and hardware stores, hotels, doctors, lumber mills, meat markets, barbershops and even an opera house.

The rooms are spacious and elegant with lots of art and accessories. Each has a queen-size bed and a private bath. There are some things they don't have, too, like televisions, which can be particularly refreshing for guests who are trying to unplug for awhile. I love the extralong tub in the Garden Room, which is original to the home, and the handsome British colonial decor in the Empire Room. The Eastlake Room has a private balcony, which overlooks the expansive front grounds.

Seven years later, to add living space for David's parents, they built the Carriage House just behind the main home, with four more glorious guest rooms plus a first-floor sitting room. Each room in the Carriage House has a king-size bed, a television, a sitting area and either a desk or a work area, plus a gas fireplace. The decor reflects David and Jim's love of travel, and they've incorporated many of their favorite styles from around the world. The Savannah Room, for example, is decidedly southern, while the Tuscany Room sports a classic Roman fountain on the wall of the huge bathroom. Jim describes the Brighton Room as "a combination of English and world traveler!"

The main floor of the Carriage House has a comfy sitting room with a gas fireplace, large TV and library of DVDs, plus a refrigerator, which the innkeepers keep stocked with snacks. Guests love to gather here after an afternoon of cross-country skiing or snowshoeing, and Jim says it the best place in the county to watch the Super Bowl!

The two buildings are joined by a covered walkway and surrounded by mature gardens and sitting areas. There are hammocks tucked here and there. The estate's original shuffleboard court is well maintained, and a small outbuilding from the home's early years has been converted into a magazine-worthy landscaped garden shed. Set back from the road on 2 ½ manicured acres, this is truly a gracious estate.

Jim begins to describe breakfast at the inn and then laughs and

Photo by Suzanne Dalton, courtesy of Bellaire Bed and Breakfast

admits that he and David are "food pushers." Let me say that you will not go hungry here. You will not even have a chance to GET hungry here! Food and beverages begin to appear about 5:00 p.m. during the inn's social hour.

"We love this time because we get to interact with our guests," says Jim. "It's a great time for guests to share stories, and often guests who just met that evening end up going out to dinner together."

When you come back after dinner, you'll find a plate of cookies waiting for you.

Breakfast is an elaborate feast that includes two juices, usually orange and something exotic like blueberry pomegranate. That could be followed by an English raisin bread pudding, a mixed fruit salad, bagels or breads, those delightful iced cherry scones and rashers of bacon. It's different every day, and accommodating vegans and those with dietary preferences is not a problem. Jim says he makes a delicious vegan hash with soy sausage, peppers, asparagus, portobello mushrooms and other veggies. He serves it with a garlic artichoke salsa. Oh my!

Besides the vistas and shops and recreation, there's another thing Jim appreciates about Bellaire. "It's filled with people who are following their passion," he says. "That creates a community with a lot of interesting small businesses—great places to eat and shop and play."

Photo by Suzanne Dalton, courtesy of Bellaire Bed and Breakfast

Vitals

rooms: 9, 5 in the main house, 4 in the Carriage House, all with private baths

pets permitted: no

pets on premises: yes, 2 lovable dogs and 2 cats, which are kept in their own quarters or outside

open season: year-round

rates: $90 to $245

email: info@bellairebandb.com

*website:*www.bellairebandb.com

owners/innkeepers:
Jim Walker and David Schulz
212 Park Street, Bellaire, MI 49615
231-533-6077
800-545-0780

BELLAIRE

The Grand Victorian
Bed and Breakfast Inn

If this remarkable home looks familiar to you, it may be because you bought a box of Post Selects during August 2006, when a photo of it graced the back of thirty-two million boxes of the popular breakfast cereal. Owners Ken and Linda Fedraw will be happy to show you one of those boxes, but they seem to take that kind of fame in stride. And that's a good thing, because The Grand Victorian regularly draws the attention of everyone from admiring travel writers to tourists stopping to take photos of it. And what is it doing in Bellaire? This gingerbread beauty, which many experts consider to be one of the finest examples of Queen Anne design in the United States, is here because of one man's plan to make a good clothespin and, of course, a promise of love.

Robert Richardi moved from Germany to the United States with his young wife in 1859. He spent a year in Pennsylvania's 177th Infantry, moved to Ohio and later settled in Missouri where he established a clothespin factory. He received patents for several wood designs and tools, and he grew wealthy. In 1881 he moved to Bellaire, took on a partner and built a large woodenware factory. Robert liked the area for its proximity to the Chain of Lakes, which were critical for shipping his products.

Amazingly, the factory was electrified—remember, it was the 1880s—by a dam located on property he purchased from a railroad company. At its peak the company employed 145 people and generated $80,000 a year in revenue.

Tragedy struck in 1887. The factory burned to the ground, and the fire claimed the life of Robert's youngest son, Charlie. Soon afterward Robert turned over his holdings in Bellaire over to his oldest son, Henry, and left the country.

Henry had a gift for business but not for love. He had met a young woman in Germany and hoped to entice her to move to Bellaire with the promise that he would build her a beautiful house. She asked that he build the house first. Fueled with anticipation, he created this stellar mansion. Henry had access to the best woods in the world and used the best woodworkers he could find, and the result is a masterpiece. Besides its ornate exterior, with arched carpenter's lace, corbels, cedar shakes, covered balconies and a square fourth-floor cupola, the home had indoor plumbing and central gravity heat. It also had electric lights—a first for a private home in northern Michigan!

Alas . . . the young lady balked at the move, or perhaps she was never really interested in joining Henry in Bellaire. We don't know her motives, but history does record that Henry was devastated. He had the house boarded up immediately.

It was eventually sold, and for nearly one hundred years it was a private residence. In 1989 it was converted to the Richardi House Bed and Breakfast, later renamed The Grand Victorian. "The condition of the home is a tribute to the fifteen owners who had this house and cared for it," says Linda. "They never painted the ornate interior wood or stripped its original features."

You can spend hours looking at the details here—oak, chestnut and

bird's-eye maple trim, delicate wood rosettes, deep bay windows dressed with ornate fretwork, crown moldings, heavy pocket doors. Henry also added Italian chandeliers, stately fireplaces, etched glass and bathrooms. Against that backdrop of original craftsmanship are reproduction Victorian wallpapers, antiques, and sweet accessories that make it feel like you've stepped back to an era of gentility.

There are two parlors and a dining room on the first floor where guests gather and relax. Four elegant, antique-filled sleeping rooms are on the second floor. It's difficult to pick a favorite, but I love the sentiment of the Blossom Room. It is named for Blossom Bacon, the only child known to have been born here. It is the original master bedroom, and the attached bathroom has the original claw-foot soaking tub.

If you love being in the midst of Victoriana but prefer accommodations that are a bit more contemporary, ask about the two second-floor suites in the carriage house that were added in the last few years. Each has Victorian touches along with a king-size bed and sitting area, a fireplace and two-person whirlpool tub in the room, and a TV with a DVD player. They have an entrance separate from the home.

Ken and Linda serve a full breakfast to guests of both the home and the carriage house, and in keeping with the grandness here, the table is set with fine china, crystal and candles. "People eat with their eyes first, so I set a pretty table, and I love to hear the oohs and aahs as guests arrive for breakfast," says Linda. "Sometimes guests run back up to their room to get their camera so they can take a picture of the table before they eat!"

Linda is the breakfast cook. She changes the menu daily, and it's clear she has fun serving elegant meals. On an early autumn day when we talked, guests were being treated to grilled peaches and cream sauce with coffee cake, quiche and buttermilk biscuits, tomatoes and potatoes. On another day, they might have strawberry scones or blueberry blintzes topped with lemon curd and powdered sugar, Richardi puff pancakes with ham and sautéed apples or eggs benedict. She can also effortlessly adapt the menu to those with special dietary needs.

Do take some time to sit and observe the goings on in Bellaire from the white wicker chairs on the wraparound porch and gazebo. And take a walk through the yard. Linda and Ken have nurtured lush gardens and tucked in quiet sitting areas, creating, perhaps, the kind of peaceful setting that Henry Richardi once dreamed he would enjoy with his new bride.

Vitals:

rooms: 6, 4 rooms in the home and 2 suites in the carriage house, all with private baths

pets permitted: no

pets in residence: none

open season: mid-April to end of November

rates: $125 to $215

e-mail: innkeeper@grandvictorian.com

website: www.grandvictorian.com

owners/innkeepers:
Linda and Ken Fedraw
402 North Bridge Street
Bellaire, MI 49615
877-438-6111

CHARLEVOIX

Horton Creek Inn
Bed and Breakfast

What comes to mind when you think about going "up north?" If your thoughts drift to the peace and quiet of deep forests, walking trails and well-tended gardens, stargazing at night and waking to the sound of birds singing and the smell of breakfast cooking, keep reading.

Horton Creek Inn is a big, contemporary cedar log home surrounded by 60 acres of Michigan pines and hardwoods. Owners Jeannie and Dave Babbitt built it in 1991, raised their four children there, then transformed their residence into a north-woods-themed inn and opened for guests in 2001. It's a piece of paradise located in the middle of the triangle formed by Charlevoix, Petoskey and Boyne City, convenient to all the cultural and recreational opportunities in this popular vacation area, yet truly away from it all. While the slopes, shops, festivals and entertainment are just a few minutes away, you may be happily tempted to never leave the grounds of the inn.

For starters there are the sleeping rooms, each decorated with a different "up-north" theme carried through in the bed quilts, pillows, artwork, lamps and wall coverings, and each has a descriptive name that tells the story. From the first-floor Garden Room, with an inviting bistro table and chairs in its bay window and a deck that overlooks lovely gardens, to the Bear Room, with a bearskin rug on the wall, each is decorated against the backdrop of warm wood, handcrafted bedsteads, big windows, French doors and beautiful views of the out of doors. Several rooms have vaulted ceilings formed by the home's tall gables, and some have a whirlpool tub or gas fireplace for extra coziness on chilly nights. The Tree Top Suite includes the Tree Top Room and Waterfowl Room, which share a sitting area and bathroom—perfect for families traveling with kids or two couples.

Each room is furnished with a CD player and a selection of instrumental music, robes, a hair dryer and toiletries, soft and firm pillows and a ceiling fan and oscillating fan. For those rare hot summer days, there is air-conditioning.

Outside your room you'll find plenty of areas to gather with friends and other guests and quiet corners where you can be alone with a good book. Throughout the inn, Jeannie and Dave have endeavored to bring the outside in, and that is especially evident in the four-season dining room with its full wall of floor-to-ceiling windows and glass roof. Breakfast is served there each morning at 9:00 a.m. If you have plans to be on your way earlier, the Babbitts will be happy to accommodate your schedule. Just let them know in advance.

Jeannie is an accomplished baker and cake decorator, but Dave is the breakfast cook, and his collection of recipes is vast. "We had guests who stayed here for twenty days," he recalls, "and they never had the same breakfast twice!" You can look forward to house specialties such as eggs benedict or upside-down banana French toast, Belgian waffles or quiche. And so you can reproduce their tempting dishes at home, the Babbitts post one of their guest-approved recipes on their website each month. You'll also find recipes for the desserts they serve each evening.

As for those 60 acres, feel free to wander the gardens, walk the trails or relax on the balcony and breathe the fresh woodland air. Horton Creek runs through the property, and you can sit on the bridge and dangle your toes in it. There's also a beautiful in-ground pool to enjoy.

Ernest Hemingway fans come to this area in search of places where their beloved writer spent time living and writing. One of Hemingway's favorite spots was a cabin located on what are now the grounds of the Horton Creek Inn. The budding writer and his friend Bill Smith, whose uncle owned the cabin, stayed there often. It was there that Hemingway was inspired to write his short story "The Three Day Blow," which opens with his popular character, Nick Adams, walking in the orchard near the cabin. Smoke is rising from its chimney, and a fall wind is blowing through the leafless trees. The story was first published in his collection *In Our Time* in 1925.

The old cabin burned down years ago, but the foundation remains, along with a few old apple trees. Dave will fill you in on the details and take you to the site.

Vitals

rooms: 7, 5 with private baths, 2 with a shared bath that can be reserved as a suite

pets permitted: no

pets in residence: none

open season: year-round

rates: $135 to $200 with a two-night minimum most weekends

e-mail: Jeannie@hortoncreekinnbb.com

website: www.hortoncreekinnbb.com

owners/innkeepers:
Jeannie and Dave Babbitt
05757 Boyne City Road
Charlevoix, MI 49720
231-582-5373
866-582-5373 for reservations

LELAND

The Riverside Inn

The first time I stayed at The Riverside Inn, it was autumn, shortly before it would close for the season. The trees were gorgeous, and it was cold. I was about seventeen, and when I checked in with my mother and father we were handed extra blankets and space heaters. We loved it! The inn was exactly the kind of rustic place we were looking for. That was in the 1960s.

Even at that point, the inn had come a long way from its earliest days. It was built on the banks of the Leland River by Jacob Schwartz to be a boathouse next door to his original Riverside Inn. Schwartz ran a popular establishment, and at the request of his guests he converted the boathouse to a dance hall just a year after it was completed. Tourists had discovered Leland, and business was good.

In 1924 a fire broke out on the third floor of the inn. The efforts of a community bucket brigade helped slow its progress long enough for most of the furnishings to be saved, but the frame building was a total loss. Undaunted, Anna and Blanche Schwartz, Jacob's daughters, who had taken over business matters when their parents died, decided to renovate the dance hall. They had the building turned so it would sit parallel to the river, and they raised the roof a half story. The following year, it opened for business as the second Riverside Inn.

In the 1980s the inn underwent a marvelous and much-needed face-lift, and then owners Barbara and Ed Collins added a dining room, which started the inn's reputation for serving great food. It has aged well over the decades.

It was a warm September morning when I last visited The Riverside Inn. A guest came in from the patio praising the "wonderful breakfast!" The light breeze drifting in off Lake Michigan promised a perfect late summer day in this picturesque village. Owner Kate Vilter was busy

taking reservations, talking with guests and attending to all the details that have made this comfortable inn a favorite place for both locals and travelers. Kate's family summered in Leland, and she started working in the hospitality industry when she was a teenager. When the inn came on the market, Kate and her mother bought it. "We thought it would be a great thing to do!" she recalls.

One of the first major expansions they undertook involved digging out the basement to make more room for wine storage and tripling the size of the kitchen. And oh, what comes out of that kitchen! Daily offerings are often purchased from local vendors, so the fish special, for example, could be locally caught, pan-roasted ruby trout served with locally harvested fingerling potatoes and beets. You could start the meal with a house-made charcuterie and an artisan cheese and continue with a pan-roasted rib eye served with truffle mac and cheese, or a house-made ravioli with English peas and chanterelle mushrooms. Kate describes the menu as global cuisine with an emphasis on local products.

I love the classic cottage look and feel of the dining areas here. The indoor rooms are two former porches with tall windows that offer views of the river, the patio and the park next door. A deck along the river offers more seating, and it's such a beautiful view that diners often choose to eat there even when it's chilly enough for a jacket. The tables

are covered with white cloths, and there are little vases of fresh flowers on each one. Residents from around Leelanau Peninsula come here to celebrate anniversaries and birthdays.

The central room has a great, square, wooden bar in the middle with extra seating areas around it. "Summer and year-round residents love to gather here and order a drink and an appetizer or sit on the dock and read a book," says Kate, who often comes here on her day off. "They like the fact that there's no TV in the bar and it's relaxed here. It lends itself to conversation. It's a great place to end the day." Most of the artwork in the inn is done by local artists represented by a nearby gallery, and it changes regularly.

Where once there were eight or ten second-floor sleeping rooms with shared baths, now there are four with private baths. Two are spacious suites that were made by combining smaller rooms, and two are the original size. Three have views of the river. Contemporary furnishings and beautiful bedsteads are blended with a few well-placed antiques, and the effect is quite charming.

Breakfast for overnight guests includes a buffet with individual quiches, a selection of breads or English muffins, cereals and fresh fruit. It's set up in the restaurant and may be eaten inside or out. Kate says the usually quiet river is a popular place for kayaking. Both kayaks and boats can be rented in town, and boats will be delivered to the Riverside's dock. Leland's quaint shops and its renowned Fishtown are just two blocks away.

"Any ghosts?," I ask.

"Yes," Kate says. "Her name is Mary Adams, and she is very nice. She just startles us once in a while. Mary was the daughter of one of the inn's early owners. We think she grew up here and is still here. The common room upstairs is named after her."

Vitals

rooms: 4 with private baths

pets permitted: no

pets in residence: none

open season: first weekend in May through the middle of December. The restaurant is closed on Tuesdays after Labor Day and open weekends only beginning in November

rates: $110 to $195

e-mail: info@theriverside-inn.com

website: www.theriverside-inn.com

owner/innkeeper:
Kate Vilter
302 River Street
Leland, MI 49654
231-256-9971
888-257-0102

Ludington House
Bed and Breakfast

Kris and Bill Stumpf bought the Ludington House after Bill retired from running metal stamping companies. Kris describes the home as having been "rather dilapidated" when they first saw it, and that's hard to picture given the elegant original features and spotless sunny rooms you'll find today. In true Victorian fashion, the home has high ceilings and beautiful polished woodwork, and the furnishings reflect the era but are toned down a bit in favor of comfort. Lace curtains on the first floor let in wonderful light from several large windows, which show off ornate cranberry-colored etched glass and the parlor's unusual fireplace mantle crafted from painted slate and inlaid marble.

All eight guest rooms are on the second and third floors, and they range in size from the spacious Wicker Room, which has two queen-size beds and a sitting area, to the cozy Skylight Room with its gorgeous raspberry-colored wallpaper and a window to the stars. The second-floor Master Suite has an in-room whirlpool tub for two and one of the home's original fireplaces. Each room has a private bath and lots of sweet pampering touches. including plush guest robes.

Bill is in charge of breakfast. "I cook like you'd expect an engineer to cook," he laughs, explaining his methodical process of writing out recipes and instructions. The food is plated and served to guests beginning about 8:30 a.m. Several small tables in the dining room seat two to four people, so couples can have tables to themselves if they wish. Guests can look forward to treats such as a German apple pancake, peach schnapps French toast and crustless quiche. Gluten-free and vegetarian options are always available with notice the night before. The Stumpfs usually spend a little time in the evening with guests who have special dietary needs so they can be sure the menu will suit them. Guests head-

Ludington

In the late 1800s, Ludington was home to many families that were amassing great wealth from business endeavors in and around the thriving lumber industry. Their homes were large—usually three floors—and were often finished with fine imported woods, leaded glass windows and sweeping staircases. Servants' quarters housed live-in staff, and carriage houses held prized horses and buggies.

This is a tale of two families. Antoine Cartier was a lumber baron who moved from Quebec to Ludington. In 1878 he built a lovely Victorian-style home on the main street, just a few blocks from Lake Michigan, where he and his wife Eliza raised eight children. Their son, Warren, attended the University of Notre Dame and came back to Ludington to join his father in business. Warren also went to the World's Columbian Exposition, better known as the Chicago World's Fair of 1893, which covered more than 600 acres and featured buildings of predominantly neoclassical design. He was so taken with the architecture that he built a neoclassical mansion for his family in 1905 across the street from the home of his parents.

More than a century later both homes have become bed-and-breakfast inns, to the delight of their guests, who get to live like wealthy community patriarchs while they visit a town known for nineteenth-century mansions, nationally ranked beaches and quaint shops. Ludington is also home to the SS *Badger*, a 1953 410-foot car ferry that makes daily trips in the summer to Manitowoc, Wisconsin.

Antoine's home is called the Ludington House Bed and Breakfast. Warren's is called the Cartier Mansion.

---

ing to the ferry for the morning crossing to Wisconsin will be served a full breakfast as well, about an hour earlier, so they can make their boarding time without having to rush.

There are at least two features in this house that Warren, son of the builders, must have liked enough to add to his own (see Cartier Mansion.) The first is a warming oven built into the radiator in the dining room. It's a brilliant design, and once you see it you'll wonder why every home in the snowbelt that was heated with radiators didn't have one! The second is a small tub, perhaps 15 inches square, with feet that match those on the large tub beside it. Some observers have thought these were tubs for bathing babies, but Kris says a little research revealed that they were designed for washing one's feet. Given that most roads were not paved when this house was built, and feet could get pretty dirty by the end of the day, it was a most practical addition to the bath. Warren apparently agreed.

Vitals

    rooms: 8 with private baths

    pets permitted: no

    pets in residence: none

    open season: year-round

    rates: $99 to $195

    e-mail: info@ludingtonhouse.com

    website: www.ludingtonhouse.com

    owners/innkeepers:
      Kris and Bill Stumpf
      501 East Ludington Avenue
      Ludington, MI 49431
      231-845-7769
      800-827-7869

LUDINGTON

Cartier Mansion

Neoclassical architecture enjoyed a long run of popularity, but most often we see it in commercial and government buildings. Standing in front of the spectacular neoclassical Cartier Mansion, I was wowed. In fact, speechless.

You can see from the photo that this inn is the definition of *grand*, and it sets the perfect stage for what you'll find inside. Original features such as rich woodwork, light fixtures, built-in buffets and sitting areas—even walls that were hand painted and stenciled—have been carefully preserved for more than one hundred years. From the welcoming foyer, you can see that Cartier's craftsmen were particularly skilled in their use of wood, and they used several varieties. The living room is finished in cherry, and there's walnut in the library. The music room features mahogany, and the dining room is paneled in sycamore. The gleaming floors in each room have unique patterns of inlaid wood as well. The effect is stunning.

There are five sleeping rooms on the second floor. They are all lovely, and each has special touches. If you want peaceful slumber surrounded by the kind of luxury that Warren Cartier and his wife enjoyed, consider the King Suite. It has a large sleeping room with a four-poster bed, a roomy sitting room and private access to the wonderful front balcony over the main entrance. The private bathroom has the original "cage" shower, a soaking tub, a unique little foot tub that is a twin to the one in the Ludington House, and a modern jetted tub.

The Blue Silk Room is sheathed in original light blue silken wall coverings. The Cottage Room features a made-for-soaking claw-foot tub right in the room.

Breakfast is hot and homemade, and guests are asked ahead of time when they would like it served. If you're planning to take the early ferry

to Wisconsin, you'll find it ready for you at 7:30 a.m., which gives you plenty of time to enjoy house specialties such as praline French toast and French-pressed coffee.

Because of the inn's sizable kitchen and liquor license, it's an ideal location for holding special events. The landscaped grounds, pergola and pristine carriage house can accommodate weddings for up to one hundred guests.

Vitals

rooms: 5 with private baths

pets permitted: no

pets in residence: none

open season: year-round

rates: $99 to $195

e-mail: info@cartiermansion.com

website: www.cartiermansion.com

owners/innkeepers:
Sue Ann and Gary Schnitker
409 East Ludington Avenue
Ludington, MI 49431
231-843-0101

OLD MISSION PENINSULA

Chateau Chantal Winery and Inn

Chateau Chantal has award-winning wines, luxurious guest rooms and inspiring views of both East and West Grand Traverse Bay from its hilltop location on the Old Mission Peninsula. And we'll get to all those good things, but first I want to tell you a story of one man's vision and a family's remarkable journey into winemaking.

Bob Begin was born in Detroit to French Canadian parents. His first language was French. He entered Sacred Heart Seminary at the eighth grade, graduated to St. John's seminary and was a Catholic priest for twelve years before deciding he wanted a different career. Nadine Grasinski became a nun and taught home economics. After twenty-two years, she, too, came to a crossroads and wanted to change her life. Bob and Nadine met in Detroit, fell in love and were married in the 1970s. A beautiful daughter followed.

Bob's dream was to create a winery in the style of a European chateau, where people could come to relax, be greeted by members of the family, drink good wines "made from the grapes outside the window" and stay overnight. In the 1980s the family moved from the Detroit area to the Old Mission Peninsula and then spent a year in Europe researching wineries.

They returned to Michigan enthused. And here's a little bit of magic . . . Bob was cross-country skiing near his house when he came upon a large cherry orchard growing on the second highest elevation on the peninsula. It was a perfect setting for growing grapes, and it was for sale. The Begins bought the land and planted their first grapevines—Chardonnay and Riesling—in 1986. In 1993 the wine was ready, and so were three bed-and-breakfast suites. Chateau Chantal, named in honor of the Begins' daughter Marie-Chantal, threw open its doors. Nadine was the breakfast cook

Ten years later the family added a wing of guest suites and expanded

Photo by Brian Confer, courtesy of Chateau Chantal

the cellar capacity to accommodate their growing wine production. Then they topped off the cellar with a glorious deck that faces the East Bay and enlarged the wine shop and tasting area. With its soaring ceilings and broad vistas, Chateau Chantal feels very much like a familial European winery perched on the top of a mountain—exactly what Bob envisioned.

"Dad is technically retired now," says Marie-Chantal with a chuckle. "But this is what he loves, so he's here doing everything all week. He is the creative entrepreneur, still. He and mom live here. Mom still makes breakfast a few days a week, and Dad is often here pouring orange juice!" Marie-Chantal is director of marketing for the winery, and her Australian-born husband, Paul Dalese, is vineyard manager.

Amid the elegance and international awards, this winecentric family strives to demystify wine, put people at ease and promote an atmosphere that is relaxed and fun. Indeed, on a warm September afternoon when I stopped by, the chateau was filled with people having a very good time!

One unique aspect of Chateau Chantal is that the inn is under the same roof as the winery. A door from the tasting room takes you into the 2,000-square-foot hospitality room where you get clear views of acres of vineyards and the bays beyond. There are tables and chairs inside and out and a sitting area with a wood-burning fireplace. A buffet breakfast is offered here each morning for guests of the inn and includes an egg

The phylloxera story
By Marie-Chantal Dalese

Growing up in the cherry and wine business presented unique opportunities when I was a student. I fondly recall the A+ I earned for a ninth-grade research report on the topic of phylloxera. Perhaps the high mark was awarded simply for undertaking a unique topic!

Phylloxera is a pest of commercial grapevines worldwide, originally native to eastern North America. These almost microscopic, pale yellow, sap-sucking insects, related to aphids, feed on the roots and leaves of grapevines. This pest had an enormous impact on the European wine grape industry in the late 1800s when an English botanist collected American grape-vines and planted them in Great Britain. The American vines were phylloxera-resistant, but they carried the pest, which spread onto the continent and destroyed most of the European wine grapes.

A significant amount of research was devoted to finding a solution to Europe's phylloxera problem, and two major options emerged: hybridization and replanting European grapevines grafted onto phylloxera-resistant American rootstocks. Who knew American grapes would first devastate, then help produce the great European wine industry!

dish, breakfast meat and fresh fruit and breads, plus Chateau Chantal's signature wine jams.

Beyond this grand room are eleven guest accommodations on two levels. They range in size from one room with a private bath to petite suites, master suites and an executive apartment that has two bedrooms, two baths, a living room with a granite fireplace and a full kitchen.

A French impressionist print hangs in each guest room, which, in turn, gives the room its name and inspires its color palette and luxurious French country furnishings. You can see photos of each one on the website. All the rooms have a wet bar and minirefrigerator. The suites each have a separate sitting room and a private patio or balcony. Many have a couch that is also a fold-out bed. Some of the bathrooms have whirlpool tubs. I was especially taken with the Morisot Suite, which includes a stunning wheelchair-accessible shower with glass French doors. If you can't decide which room you like best, consider your preference for sunrises or sunsets. Both are awesome here. There's a small exercise room for guests to use as well, and you'll have a fine view of the

West Bay as you log miles on the treadmill.

Adult overnight guests receive a complimentary glass of wine at check-in and a complimentary wine tasting. With wine production running at eighteen to twenty thousand cases a year, you don't have to worry about supplies running low. The original 40 acres of grapes are situated on a 65-acre estate, and another 45 acres of grapes are grown elsewhere on the peninsula. The owners also have a 55-acre vineyard in Argentina where they grow Malbec grapes, which are crushed and shipped as bulk wine to the winery, where it is bottled and finished.

Photo by Brian Confer, courtesy Chateau Chantal

Chateau Chantal is a certified green lodging, meaning it follows specific practices that save energy and protect the environment. It has received the Michigan Agriculture Environmental Assurance Program verification by the Michigan Department of Agriculture, signifying its commitment to environmental stewardship and sustainable business practices. The staff is passionate about recycling everything from glass bottles and cardboard to the skins and seeds of the pressed grapes, which are turned into compost and put back into the soil. In fact that grape-rich compost and manure are the only fertilizers used on the grapes. "It makes sense," says Marie-Chantal. "To create the best wine, we need to nurture the soil."

If you want a great way to experience Chateau Chantal and don't have time for a stay at the inn, check the website for the schedule of wine dinners and cooking classes held here throughout the year. You'll eat well and learn how to pair the winery's products with various foods. Or come for tapas tours and sunset jazz in the summer.

While the inn's busy season is spring to fall, consider a visit in the winter, which could look like this: a gentle snow falling, the fireplaces blazing, and you, warm and relaxed with a glass of Chateau Chantal's famed Late Harvest Riesling or its lovely sparkling wine called Tonight. Ahhh . . .

Vitals

rooms: 10 rooms and suites with private baths, 1 apartment with 2 bedrooms and 2 baths

pets permitted: no

pets in residence: none

open season: year-round except Christmas Day, New Year's Day and Easter Sunday

rates: $155 to $295 for a room or suite, $405 to $550 for the executive apartment

e-mail: wine@chateauchantal.com

website: www.chateauchantal.com

owners/innkeepers:
Bob and Nadine Begin
15900 Rue de Vin
Traverse City, MI 49686
231-223-4110
800-969-4009

OLD MISSION PENINSULA

The Inn at Chateau
Grand Traverse

Part of the fun of staying at this inn, besides being surrounded by acres of orchards and grapevines and just a minute's walk from the tasting room, is that it's small and luxurious and feels like your own private resort. It's tucked into a hillside on the grounds of the estate and blends beautifully into the landscape, so if you didn't know to look for it, you might miss it.

Each of the six roomy suites has a king- or queen-size bed and a sitting area with a pull-out sofa, private bath, and private balcony. They were remodeled in 2012, and they are lovely. In fact you might be tempted to stay in your room while you're here because it has everything you need for a restful retreat, including a small refrigerator, microwave and coffeemaker. I also like the clever suite names—Wine at the Beach is my favorite.

Do come out of your room, though, because there is so much to this inn beyond your door. The huge living room has a U-shaped couch in front of a fireplace, and there's an airy sun-room, which just might be the perfect place to enjoy a glass of wine on a warm afternoon. From both rooms there are panoramic views of vineyards and orchards and Grand Traverse Bay. Sliding doors take you out onto a large wraparound balcony where the views get even better.

There's more. Off the living room is a formal dining area with a magnificent walnut and cherry table that seats sixteen. This is where chef-prepared dinners with wine pairings are held throughout the year. You can check the website for dates.

On the lower level, you'll find an exercise room with state-of-the-art

Grapes and growing conditions

If you've wondered why this region is growing great wine grapes, here is a bit of the story. European vinifera vines, which is what Chateau Grand Traverse has planted, require specific growing conditions, and this unique region of microclimates obliges. The mass of water in Grand Traverse Bay that encircles the Old Mission Peninsula moderates temperatures, protecting the vines from potential frost in the spring, extending the ripening period in the fall, and creating more than 120 inches of snow in winter, which reduces vine damage.

equipment, a sauna, a game room, cable TV, more room for kicking back in front of another fireplace, and a laundry room for guests. Another set of sliding doors leads to a ground-floor patio. The lines throughout are clean and contemporary, the furnishings are chic and comfortable, and it's all set against a backdrop of those amazing vistas.

Breakfast is very casual here. It usually includes breads and cereals, individual quiches, hard-cooked eggs, juice and fruit and make-your-own waffles. It's all stocked in the refrigerator in the breakfast room, and you can help yourself whenever you're hungry. A complimentary bottle of Chateau Grand Traverse wine is included with each night of your stay.

"Guests can interact as much or as little as they want while they're here," says Eddie O'Keefe, whose father, Edward O'Keefe Jr., started the winery in 1974. "If they need something, we're just a call away." The winery is still family owned—Edward lives on site.

After giving me a tour of the guest quarters, Eddie pushed on a section of wall on the lower level. Just like in a gothic movie, it opened, and we walked into a very large room that looks every bit like a secret hall in a castle. It's called the Prohibition Room—a great name, given that it is undetectable when that door is shut. With its vaulted ceiling and arches, slate and wood floors, tapestries and ironwork, it is pure Old World. It is available for special events, and it might be worth your while to invent one just so you can hold it here!

Chateau Grand Traverse is the oldest and largest commercial winery and vineyard operation in northern Michigan. At maximum capacity, the winery can press 50 tons of grapes a day and produces about one hundred thousand cases of wine each year. Eddie takes pride in the

practices they have adopted at the winery to work in harmony with the environment. It has earned recognition in the Michigan Agriculture Environmental Assurance Program for operating with the highest environmental standards set by the State of Michigan. For example, Chateau Grand Traverse has eliminated the use of pre-emergent herbicides in its 122 acres of estate-owned vineyards and has a program to rebuild the soil using compost and organic material. Cover crops decrease soil erosion and increase beneficial insects and birds. The crew is also in the process of transitioning a 20-acre vineyard to meet organic standards.

The installation of thirty-five bird, bat and predator houses has created a habitat that is now home to more than forty-five bird species. Integrated pest management is practiced to reduce or eliminate the use of pesticides. All glass bottles and corrugated materials generated at the winery are recycled. All winemaking equipment and production facilities are cleaned and sanitized by means of ozone, steam and other environmentally safe methods.

The list of wines currently available is long, and the list of medals won by the wines is impressive. The winery bottles under four brands, including Traverse Bay Winery, which produces cherry wine and cherry wine blends made from northern Michigan fruit. You can learn about all the wines by going to the website and downloading the winery information packet. But it's a whole lot more fun to go to the tasting room!

Vitals

rooms: 6 with private baths

pet permitted: no

pets in residence: you might run into a winery dog or two, but they are not permitted in guest quarters

open season: year-round

rates: $125 to $200

e-mail: info@cgtwines.com

website: www.cgtwines.com

owners/innkeepers:
The O'Keefe family
12301 Center Road
Traverse City, MI 49686
800-283-0247

PENTWATER

Hexagon House

The curious hexagon was introduced as a style for homes in America shortly before the Civil War, and it seems to have been pretty much forgotten after the war. It was not an easy structure to build, and it created small inside corners that could make furniture placement difficult. But architects praised the design because it offered abundant opportunities to bring in natural light. The central cupola, with its six windows, was often positioned over the staircase, flooding the interior of the home with light in the way that we use skylights today, and it acted as a vent to draw in fresh air and cool the rooms on warm days. Several twentieth-century urban planners championed hexagonal designs for the layout of residential subdivisions.

History does not record why S. E. Russell chose the hexagon when he constructed this building in the 1870s, but we do know he used it as a boardinghouse for lumbermen who came to Pentwater to buy wood. Early photos show that it remained a simple two-story, six-sided building until the 1990s when a remarkable transformation took place. An old garage was removed and replaced with a nearly hidden two-car garage and a large first-floor family room. And 4,000 square feet of Victorian-style porches were added to the first and second floors, completely encircling the hexagon and matching the original building so perfectly that visitors seeing the inn for the first time assume it has looked this way from the beginning. All that gracious architecture sits back from the road on 3 acres of lush lawn and gardens, and it's quite stunning!

Matt and Sandy Werner's love affair with inns goes back to 1988 when they were married at the Montague Inn in Saginaw, Michigan. Purchasing the Hexagon House was a dream come true, and remarkably, they are only its sixth owners.

While a hexagon might seem a bit of a challenge to furnish, given those extra angles, you'll see no hint of that here. Each room is bright

and welcoming, and the five guest rooms are lovely. If you're celebrating a special occasion or plan to settle in for a few days, consider reserving the first-floor Cottage Rose Suite. Decorated in soft yellows and white, it's one of the prettiest rooms I've seen. I love it all, from the king-size bed and large sitting area to the white cabinetry, walk-in closets and beautiful bathroom with a jetted tub. And it has a door leading to the porch. The four guest rooms on the second floor offer some fun options in decor, which vary from the romantic pink and white Cherub Room to the lodgelike Homestead Room with its earthy colors and antique oak furnishings. Each room has a private bath and a door that opens onto the second-floor porch.

If the weather turns cool or downright cold, there's a cozy parlor, which you'll see as soon as you walk into the inn, and a fireplace to take off the chill. And then there's the marvelous, airy family room that was added in the 1990s with its banks of windows on three sides. It's a great place to relax and read or to gather if you're traveling with friends.

A fabulous and filling breakfast is plated and served at 9:00 a.m., and it often includes the house favorite: honey Dutch baby. For the uninitiated, this rich dish looks like cornbread baked in a pan, stuffed with cream cheese and topped with a berry sauce. Oh my! Matt says it's best fresh from the oven, but it will be kept warm if you sleep late, so you won't miss it. You're welcome to dine inside at the big table in the family room or at one of the bistro tables on the porches. Coffee, tea, sodas and dessert are always available, and if Sandy's Scotcheroos are on the buffet, do try one. Or two! They are her version of a seven-layer bar, and they are delicious.

There are several sweet traditions here in the evening. First, there is sunset. Matt says half the people in town make their way to Mears State Park to watch the sun disappear into Lake Michigan, and most will be there with an ice cream cone in hand. Back at the inn, Matt will build a bonfire outside for guests who want to pull up the Adirondack-style chairs, make s'mores and ease into the evening.

"People talk about how quiet it is here," he says, and it is indeed a peaceful getaway, set back from the street, surrounded by trees, yet just six blocks from Pentwater's bustling little downtown. The inn and the grounds lend themselves perfectly to small family reunions and weddings, and Sandy and Matt enlist the services of a local caterer who can provide everything from appetizers to multiple-course meals.

If you're a musician and you happen to be staying at the inn on a Thursday night in the summer, bring your instrument and join the core of community musicians who play at the band shell each week. Anyone who shows up is welcome to play.

And, by the way, Matt says there's no ghost at the inn. If you hear a spooky noise on a windy night, it's likely just Rodney, the rooster on the weather vane.

Vitals

rooms: 5 with private baths

pets permitted: no

pets in residence: none

open season: mid-March to mid-December

rates: $119 to $245

e-mail: innkeepers@hexagonhouse.com

website: www.hexagonhouse.com

owners/innkeepers:
Sandy and Matt Werner
760 Sixth Street
PO Box 778
Pentwater, MI 49449
231-869-4102

Stafford's Bay View Inn

A bit of sweet history about Stafford's Bay View Inn makes for a good story. Late in the 1950s, Stafford Smith was working his way through the ranks of the Bay View Inn, which sat on a prime plot of land tucked between the Bay View community and Little Traverse Bay. It had been built in 1886 and offered fifty-eight second- and third-floor rooms to guests from late June through Labor Day.

In the fall of 1960, its owner, Dr. Roy Heath, put the Bay View up for sale, and Stafford landed a position as assistant manager at the nearby Perry Hotel in Petoskey. But the Perry was sold four months later, and there was Stafford, engaged to marry Bay View Inn hostess Janice Johnson and out of a job. Undaunted, he put together a plan, approached Dr. Heath, and by spring he and Janice were innkeepers of the Bay View. In 2011 the Smith family celebrated fifty years of owning and caring for this wonderful inn and its guests.

Early guests at the Bay View Inn often stayed several weeks during the summer while they attended cultural programs in the nearby Bay View community. Many arrived in Petoskey from Cincinnati by train. By the time inns and bed-and-breakfast homes were enjoying a resurgence in popularity in Michigan around the 1980s, Stafford already had decades of innkeeping under his belt. As the years rolled along, he watched the makeup of guests change, along with their expectations. Continuous renovating and redecorating have kept Stafford's Bay View Inn fresh and stylish. Each update has added a little more comfort and elegance. Stafford chuckles when he talks about caring for a 125-year-old inn. "I have a full-time painter," he admits. "He paints outside in the summer and inside in the winter!"

There are thirty-one guest rooms now. Each is decorated in a comfortable cottage Victorian style, and some of the original rooms have been combined to create spacious suites. They vary in features from the pretty Primrose Rooms with period furnishings and private baths to the more lavish Aster Suites, which have both a sleeping room and an adjoining sitting room, a fireplace, a private bath, a whirlpool tub for two and a view of the bay. In each guestroom, you'll find antique and reproduction bedsteads, beautiful linens and wall coverings and fine toiletries. A library on the second floor is stocked with games and books plus coffee and tea service, and there's a sitting area on the third floor as well. To preserve the historic character of the inn, TVs are located only in the Sun Room and Library.

I love this sentence from the inn's website: "We welcome children of all ages as our very special guests." While many innkeepers appropriately stress that their lodgings are not suited to the needs of children, Stafford's Bay View Inn encourages families. "One of the things we have here is a lot of public space," says Stafford. "If you have a child who is crying or having a bad day, there is always a place on the porch or a nook or cranny where you and the child can go and have some quiet time." Cribs and high chairs are available, too.

The inn also takes great care to accommodate guests with disabilities. There is a ramp from the parking lot, and you can take either the stairs or an elevator to the second and third floors. Common areas of the inn are accessible by wheelchair, and two wheelchair-accessible guest rooms have walk-in showers.

The Bay View Inn's long-standing reputation for good food reflects years of perfecting recipes and the staff's ongoing attention to quality. The inn serves three meals a day, and the dining room is open to the public. Overnight guests are given a generous voucher for breakfast so they can order right from the mouthwatering menu house specialties such as Michigan cherry French toast, eggs benedict, a daily quiche, and a yogurt parfait layered with fruit and granola.

Dinner includes regional specialties such as chilled cherry soup and morel bisque, plus the inn's signature planked whitefish, a wonderful dish that has been on the menu since 1961. If you visit the area in the summer, try to get to the inn for what has become known as Stafford's Famous Sunday Brunch. It's a tradition here and a favorite of guests and locals alike. And you'll usually find Stafford there welcoming everyone.

It was a sweet surprise when Stafford called on a warm summer morning to give me an update on the inn and the other business adventures that he has embarked on in the last several years. Remember the old Perry Hotel where he was working in 1960? He bought and renovated it, and it's gorgeous. It anchors one corner of downtown Petoskey and adds much to the community. His newest project has been opening Stafford's Crooked River Lodge and Suites, a grand family-friendly log lodge in Alanson. And do ask about his wonderful restaurants!

Vitals

rooms: 31 with private baths

pets permitted: no

pets in residence: none

open season: year-round

rates: $99.00 to $319.00

e-mail: bayviewinn@staffords.com

website: www.staffords.com/bayview

owners/innkeepers:
Janice and Stafford Smith, owners
Corey Ernst, innkeeper
2011 Woodland Avenue
Petoskey, MI 49770
231-347-2771

PRUDENVILLE

Springbrook Inn

Springbook Inn was a wonderful find, and I thank my friends at the Roscommon Area District Library for telling me about it. They knew about the inn because *everybody* for miles around knows about this gem! It was a chilly day in February when I stopped by, and even though I was looking for it as I drove south on M-55, I missed it on my first pass. The inn sits back a bit from the road, and while the front is attractive, you get no hint of what's in store when you step inside.

The entrance opens into a two-story lobby and living room, with an airy vaulted ceiling and an entire wall of wood that has been hand carved with the stylized design of a tree. This is the hub of the inn. First-floor guest rooms are straight ahead. Second-floor rooms are reached by a wide, open staircase, and the East Bay Grille, offering casual fine dining, is just off the lobby to the right. The inn looked particularly festive when I walked in. Valentine's Day was a few days away, and a 20-foot-tall Christmas tree had been transformed for cupid's holiday with red hearts and ribbons.

Matt and Kathy Grover have owned this lovely four-season getaway since 2001. Matt is an inspired chef who loves feeding people good food. Kathy has traveled the world and has a great sense of design and comfort. They believe in the benefits of rest, relaxation and romance, and they created an inn that encourages all that and more.

The biggest surprise about Springbrook is the "backyard." It's 5 acres of woods and wildlife, perennial gardens and a landscaped pond stocked with Koi. All eight sleeping rooms—three on the first floor and five on the second—overlook that serene view, and each has a balcony that invites long, lazy mornings with a cup of coffee and a book. Each room also has a fireplace and a couch or overstuffed chairs, a perfectly sized bistro table and chairs, a large jetted tub and king-size bed, a private bath with luxurious towels, and Wi-Fi. Ah . . . sweet comfort!

A Lily Pad

Can't get to Prudenville this weekend? Kathy and Matt share this recipe for one of their signature drinks at The Frog that you can make at home. They call it a Lily Pad.

Take one highball glass. Fill with ice.

Add:

1 ounce Hpnotiq (a blue liqueur made of tropical fruit juices, vodka and cognac)
1 ounce coconut rum
Top off with pineapple juice. Garnish with pineapple and orange slices and a cherry.

Each room is named for outdoor landmarks—some real and some pure poetry—and each is uniquely decorated and furnished. I'm partial to the Hartwick Pines Room with its deep terra-cotta walls, which set off an elegant sleigh bed. The Springbrook Room has a romantic four-poster bed and a beautiful armoire. From amenities to furnishings and food, Kathy and Matt have paid great attention to the details, and that's a big part of what makes this inn so appealing. You don't even have to leave your room for breakfast as it's delivered right to your door in the morning—hot, fragrant, and filling.

I recommend you arrive at Springbrook in time to begin your visit with dinner in the East Bay Grille. It, too, overlooks that beautiful wooded setting. Matt's specialties include char-grilled steaks, seafood, and fish. Entrees are served with several sides, including salad, soup, fresh vegetables, and a choice of potato. Vegetarians can opt for a pasta dish or a selection of side dishes. Given a little notice, Matt will do his best to accommodate dietary preferences, and he's completely familiar with gluten-free options.

For a really fun treat, head to the inn's outdoor tiki bar, called The Frog, just a few steps from the restaurant. It features a good grille menu with sandwiches and burgers, salads, Tiki Torch Nachos, and Jimmy Buffet pouring out of the speakers. Local residents love it, and it became a popular summer hangout as soon as Kathy and Matt opened it. A few years ago, they asked themselves why they should limit its hours to the warm months. With a little ingenuity, they found a way to make The

Frog weather tight and warm, despite abundant snow and bitter cold winter temperatures in this region, and now they keep it open year-round. It's filled with all the lanterns, parrots and palm trees you have come to expect in tiki bars, and it's not uncommon to see locals pull up on their snowmobiles.

On some weekends when the music is live, or when the inn hosts special events like the hilarious Cheeseburger in Paradise feast, the music can be loud and late, so plan your visit accordingly. If you're ready to party Margaritaville style and you're looking forward to spending the evening with a plastic lei around your neck, check the website for upcoming events. And if, in the middle of winter, you find yourself in the land of deep snow, wishing for a piña colada in a steamy tiki bar, drop by The Frog. You can shed your snowmobile suit when you get inside.

Recreational activities go year-round here, and Higgins and Houghton Lakes are nearby. Whether you golf, fish, ski or boat, love the snow or prefer music festivals and county fairs, you'll find a full calendar of fun.

Vitals

rooms: 8 with private baths

pets permitted: no

pets in residence: none

open season: The inn is open year-round. The restaurant is open for dinner Wednesday through Saturday in summer and Thursday through Saturday the rest of the year.

rates: $169 to $229

e-mail: info@springbrookinn.com

website: www.springbrookinn.com

owners/innkeepers:
Kathy and Matt Grover
565 W. West Branch Road (M-55)
PO Box 390
Prudenville, MI 48651
989-366-6347

SUTTONS BAY

The Inn at Black Star Farms

When Black Star Farms' owner, Don Coe, spotted a 1990s Mount Vernon–like mansion for sale in Suttons Bay many years ago, he envisioned it as an elegant inn nestled against the Leelanau Peninsula's rolling hills and fertile farms. He saw himself as an innkeeper. He didn't see himself as a winemaker. That came later, and with good reason. This region has superb soil and weather conditions for growing wine grapes, and Don's business partner, Kerm Campbell, was looking for a place to build a winery and plant more grapes. Today the inn is surrounded by acres of vineyards, and the accolades earned by Black Star Farms' wines over the years demonstrate what happens when you marry the skills of good winemakers and great grapes.

In addition to its fine wines, Black Star Farms takes pride in its commitment to serving "local" food. Nearly 100 percent of the food prepared here is raised on its 160 acres or within 100 miles of the farm. The eggs you have for breakfast, for example, are gathered from the hens that graze next to the turkeys, across from the sheep and Mangalitsa pigs, and just down the lane from the culinary garden, which you'll pass on your way to the tasting room. Vegetables come from a type of greenhouse called a hoop house. Meats and sausages made from the animals raised here are cured here.

Members of the staff at Black Star Farms are proud of the way their animals are raised. They encourage you to visit them, and you can bet that their healthy and respectful living conditions produce superior quality meat, poultry and eggs.

It might seem odd to begin a narrative about an inn by writing about the animals that live there, but raising and serving excellent food is an integral part of this farm. And when you see the attention paid to the quality of the lives of the animals here, it's easy to understand why

everything, from the immaculately kept grounds to the sophisticated guest rooms, is top notch.

Black Start Farms was named for the striking black compass rose imbedded in the white marble floor of the mansion's foyer. You'll see it as soon as you enter. The star was also the inspiration behind naming the rooms after constellations. If you arrive at the inn by 5:30 p.m., you can join other guests in the Pegasus Lounge, just off the foyer, for hospitality hour. You'll be treated to Black Star Farms' wines, appetizers and cheeses from the Leelanau Cheese Company, which operates on the property. The lounge feels like a cozy English pub, and there's a wonderful fireplace to gather around. I imagine it's a popular place for guests after a day of cross-country skiing.

Guest rooms are on the first and second floors, and they vary greatly in both size and amenities. The first-floor Mira Suite, for example, includes a full kitchen and a sitting area with a fireplace. It's a great choice if you're planning an extended stay. Polaris, also on the first floor, has a private outside entry, a king-size bed and assistance bars in the bathroom, making it especially accommodating if you have mobility concerns. There is a daybed, too, which will sleep one extra person.

For maximum pampering, consider Diadem, named for the brightest star in the constellation Coma Berenices or Berenice's Hair. This is the home's original master suite, and it's furnished with a gorgeous king-

Recycling soap and plastic

The Inn at Black Star Farms participates in a program called Clean the World, which collects soap and shampoo products discarded from the hospitality industry—yes, those little bottles of fancy stuff that you use once and leave in the shower. Clean the World recycles them into new bars of soap and shampoo. It then distributes them to domestic homeless shelters and impoverished people around the world, helping prevent millions of deaths caused by hygiene-related illnesses.

Clean the World has put back in use more than 11 million bars of soap and 325,000 pounds of shampoo and conditioner, supporting healthy lives and simultaneously eliminating over 700 tons of waste. Learn more at www.cleantheworld.org.

size iron bed and comfortable armchairs positioned perfectly in front of a massive white marble fireplace. The luxurious bathroom has twin pedestal sinks and a very large shower. It's all quite grand.

Lyra is the smallest of the rooms and very pretty. It's tucked in a gable and has a minifridge, coffeemaker and microwave oven.

All the guest rooms are individually decorated with contemporary furnishings, designer fabrics and down comforters. Guests love the sheets so much that the inn now sells them. You'll find handcrafted chocolates in your room that are made by a Grand Haven chocolatier using Black Star Farms' fruit brandies. And you'll receive a special reserve wine tasting and a bottle of Black Star Farms Red House wine. If the cold winds blow, you can warm up in the sauna on the second floor.

The chef-prepared breakfast usually includes fresh fruit and the inn's homemade granola, an entrée with seasonal items such as cauliflower grits with farm-made sausage, corn sauté and a poached egg. The first-floor kitchen is open to the dining room so you can watch while your meal is prepared. White tablecloths and napkins are standard. With its beamed ceiling, brick-hearth-like wall, a wonderful Round Oak wood-burning stove and large windows overlooking the grounds, the room feels almost castlelike. Occasionally remind yourself that this was once a private home!

Dinners by reservation are offered here on many weekends. The menu changes with the season, and the schedule is posted on the website. The five-course harvest series and morel mushroom dinners are especially popular. The inn supports the Great Lakes Culinary Institute, and interns from the school are often cooking side by side with the chefs.

If you're looking for a quick meal, duck in to the Hearth and Vine, a small café on site that specializes in traditional wood-fired pizzas and, of course, seasonal specialties made from ingredients harvested at Black Star or nearby farms.

Black Star Farms has an excellent equestrian facility on site, as well. Guests staying at the inn are welcome to trailer their horses to the farm, board them at the stable and ride them on trails that wind through the woods and nearby countryside. There's also a large indoor arena for their use.

Vitals

rooms: 10 with private baths

pets: no

pets on premises: an occasional winery dog or two, but they are not allowed in the guest rooms

open season: year-round, except the first two weeks in January

rates: $150 to $395

e-mail: innkeeper@blackstarfarms.com

website: www.BlackStarFarms.com

owner: Don Coe

innkeepers:
Kellie Parks and Jill Ryan
10844 E. Revold Road
Suttons Bay, MI 49682
231-944-1251

TRAVERSE CITY

Antiquities Wellington Inn

When I drove up to the Antiquities Wellington Inn on a pretty September afternoon, I had to stop and catch my breath. W. Cary Hull began building this stately neoclassical mansion in 1905. It took three years to complete, which is understandable given the quality of workmanship and architectural details and its three full floors of living space. Even in a neighborhood with block after block of historic mansions, it stands out.

Cary was the son of Henry Hull, a lumber baron who owned the Oval Wood Dish Company in Traverse City. In the early 1900s, meat came packaged for the cook or lady of the house on a paper-thin sheaf of wood—oval wood—much like our Styrofoam trays today. When the meat was consumed, the dish was used to start a fire in the wood stove. They were made to be disposable, so although millions of them were made, only a few examples remain. Cary joined his father in the business. At its peak, their factory employed 325 people and consumed 15 million board feet of wood annually.

As you may know, the supply of wood in Michigan, once thought to be inexhaustible, ran out. And that was bad news for the Oval Wood Dish Company. Undaunted, Henry made plans to move his factory to Tupper Lake, New York, where standing timber was still plentiful. He also offered work at the new location to many of his employees. In one day, a two-hundred-car train pulled into Traverse City, loaded up the company owners and their families, equipment and transportable elements of the business, and fifty additional Traverse City families and headed for New York. The loss of both the business and so many residents devastated the local economy. Cary Hull's house was vacant for ten years, and when it was finally purchased, it was converted to apartments.

That might well have been the end of the story. Dividing a mansion into separate living spaces can be pretty tough on it. But when Barb Rishel toured the home in 1999, she could see that many of the opulent

features built into the house decades earlier were still in place. And Barb knew what to look for. This is the fourteenth house she has renovated. It is also the largest. This one took her four years.

"I like buildings with tall ceilings!" she told me, as we stood in the grand entrance. She also likes to keep things as original as possible. Armed with a true treasure, the home's original floor plans, Barb went room to room, saving everything she could, including wide crown moldings and a lovely thistle design stenciled on the walls that you see when you walk in the front door. To the right of the entrance is the library, which has original dark wainscoting and a beamed ceiling. To the left is the living room with a round bay of windows and a grand piano. Straight ahead is the dining room, which also has a beamed ceiling, and, remarkably, the original art glass light fixtures.

Eight bedchambers are located on the second and third floors, and as you might expect from the size of this home, most are very large. They are furnished with Victorian era antiques, including elegant vintage parlor sets, all harking back to the days when the Hulls lived there. I love the ornate, 1865 Renaissance revival black walnut bed in the Munson Chamber, which is paired with button-tufted English armchairs of the same period. There is a fireplace as well, and a door to a private balcony at the front of the house. The bathroom has the original pedestal tub and sink. The Woolsey Suite is a favorite of brides. It has a fireplace and a private balcony as well. The adjoining bath has a two-person whirlpool tub.

I was most touched by restoration work in the room that was once Jane Hull's playroom. It is called the Corbett Suite, named for American artist Bertha Corbett, whose popular Sunbonnet Babies were featured around the turn of the century on everything from the pages of children's books to china and postcards. Barb's workmen discovered part of an original Sunbonnet mural in this room. They located the outline of the entire mural, and the illustrations were meticulously re-created.

The third floor of the home is huge and open and was likely a favorite entertainment area for the Hull family. The ceiling soars to seventeen feet, and there is a small performers' balcony where musicians played while guests danced. The room is usually set up as a gathering area for overnight guests. There's a large TV with a seating area, and that still leaves plenty of room in which to practice yoga or dance! This great space is part of what makes the inn perfect for holding special events. Tables and chairs can be set up for meals, and there is an adjacent catering kitchen. There are two bedchambers on the third floor, including the Milliken Room, which has two full-size beds.

All of the rooms have lovely lamps, artwork and Victorian accessories that Barb has picked up over the years. She loves to peruse antique

shops looking for appropriate vintage goods, including fabrics. Do take a look at the draperies. Many are antique.

When she completed the restoration of the home, Barb turned her attention to the two-story carriage house and converted the second floor into two apartments. Each has a kitchen and living room. One is furnished à la 1930s art deco with two bedrooms and two baths. The adorable 1940s French country apartment has two bedrooms and one bath. Both are filled with vintage accessories and loaded with charm.

Breakfast is served at 9:00 a.m. in the first-floor dining room at tables set for four. It's plated and includes house specialties such as a Tex-Mex dish, stuffed French toast or a quiche du jour. Barb is often joined in the kitchen by interns from the Great Lakes Culinary Institute. Breakfast is not included for guests in the carriage house apartments, but they can add it if they wish.

The shops and restaurants and Traverse City's trendy downtown are within walking distance. If you're thinking about an off-season trip north, consider staying at the Wellington on Halloween. Barb says the home is visited by about twelve hundred trick-or-treaters, and her overnight guests love to help hand out candy!

Vitals

> *rooms:* 8 rooms in the house and 2 apartments in the carriage house
>
> *pets permitted:* no
>
> *pets in residence:* none
>
> *open season:* year-round
>
> *rates:* $170 to $195
>
> *e-mail:* stay@wellingtoninn.com
>
> *website:* www.wellingtoninn.com
>
> *owner/innkeeper:*
> Barb Rishel
> 230 Wellington Street
> Traverse City, MI 49686
> 231-922-9900
> 877-968-9900

WALLOON LAKE VILLAGE

Walloon Lake Inn

Ernest Hemingway loved Walloon Lake, and perhaps the first time you visit there it will be to follow in some of the footsteps of this American literary hero. If you take the time to have dinner at the Walloon Lake Inn, and even to spend a night or two, David Beier believes you will come back for the food, the remarkably clear waters of the lake, and the seductive quiet of this gentle resort area.

David is innkeeper, chef and proprietor of the Walloon Lake Inn, a venerable old structure that has served up hospitality for around one hundred years. It began its life as Fern Cottage and served as a docking point for the steamboats that transported travelers to hotels or cottages on the lake. David's emphasis here is the food he serves, and from all accounts, year after year, it is splendid—fresh, seasonal and local when possible. The inn is open for dinner pretty much seven days a week year-round, and David's menu is wonderfully creative, so arrive hungry!

For starters, consider the chef's charcuterie plate, which is a selection of rillettes or sausages made on the premises, or skillet-seared pot stickers in a citrus ginger broth served with mango and pineapple chow chow. You might also try a classic coquille saint jacques or grilled and marinated artichokes. Many of the appetizers seem hearty enough for a meal, but save room for an entrée such as mussels Walloonia, a roast half duck with apples and shallots, sautéed walleye or the chef's vegetable selection.

Then, of course, there are tempting desserts, including maple crème caramel, which features the inn's own maple syrup. And to round out the meal, choose from a selection of ports and cognacs.

David has family members with food issues, so he is well versed in making adjustments as needed. "We always have a vegetarian entrée, and if a guest wants a vegan meal, we can do that," he says. "Most of the food we serve is made right here. We know exactly what goes into

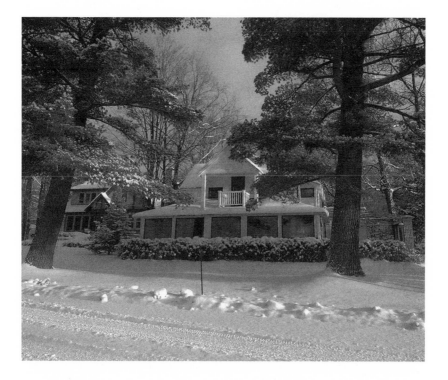

it, and most of the menu does not have wheat in it, so avoiding gluten isn't a problem."

You can count on the menu changing a bit from season to season. David posts it on the inn's website, so you can see what he's offering when you visit.

If you want to learn some of the secrets of David's appealing dishes, ask about two- and four-day classes at his Fons du Cuisine Cooking School. David teaches techniques rather than the cooking of specific dishes, so you learn skills rather than recipes. And you learn by preparing several foods, which you then get to eat! If you sign on for a class in April or May, you might be fortunate enough to cook with the elusive morels, if they happen to be appearing in northern Michigan at the time.

Classes are kept to a maximum of six students, so it's a completely hands-on experience for each person, and you'll get plenty of personal attention and time to talk about the processes.

On the second floor of the inn are five quaint and comfortable sleeping rooms. Each has a private bath, and some have a sink in the sleeping room as was customary in turn-of-the-century inns. They share a sitting area that overlooks the lake, and that's where you'll find a continental

Ernest Hemingway slept . . .

. . . at Windemere, the childhood summer home of the Hemingway family on the north shore of Walloon Lake. The original cottage was built in 1899 for $400 and measured 20 feet by 40 feet. It had two small bedrooms, a tiny kitchen and no electricity or plumbing. But there was a large fireplace, in front of which Ernest's sister Carol was born in the summer of 1911. A porch dining room and kitchen wing, plus a three-bedroom annex out back where the older children and housekeeper slept, were added later.

Family members say that Hemingway's parents chose that site, with its 260 feet of shoreline, because there was no drop off in the lake and they felt it would be safe for the children.

The family arrived at the cottage each summer after a lengthy trip. They boarded a steamship in Chicago and traveled to Harbor Springs, where they caught a train to Petoskey. In Petoskey they changed trains and rode another into the village of Walloon, where a boat took them to a public dock. There a farmer picked up the family with their summer's worth of belongings and transport everyone to the cottage. Ernest's father Clarence, a doctor, likely traveled back and forth between northern Michigan and Chicago.

It's believed that the last time Hemingway visited the cottage, as recorded by his guestbook signature, was on his honeymoon with Hadley Richardson on September 3, 1921.

buffet every morning. It includes baked goods, fresh fruit and cereals, plus "exceptionally good coffee," which comes from a local roaster. There is a fine swimming area in front of the inn, plus a dock where you can throw in a line if you wish. Diners often come to the inn by boat and tie up there.

There is much to do here twelve months of the year, and it's great that the inn is open nearly year-round, because winter at the lake is particularly quiet and wonderful. There are lots of groomed cross-country ski trails nearby, and when the lake is frozen, you can ski on it, too!

Vitals

rooms: 5 with private baths

pets permitted: usually no, but sometimes in the off-season

pets in residence: none

open season: year-round with periodic closings in spring and fall

rates: $96 summer, $65 off-season (the inn's menu and prices are on the website)

e-mail: info@walloonlakeinn.com

website: www.walloonlakeinn.com

owner/innkeeper:
David Beier
P.O. Box 459
Walloon Lake Village, MI 49796
231-535-2999
800-956-4665

Silent Sport Lodge Wilderness Bed and Breakfast

Take one fine piece of land lying lengthwise along a blue ribbon trout stream. Add one contemporary, custom-built log home and two personable outdoor enthusiasts who migrated to this tranquil location from downstate and happen to be good cooks and you have the makings for a great bed and breakfast. Add opportunities for hiking, cross-country skiing, kayaking, fishing, bicycling, bird-watching and snowshoeing and you have a vacation paradise.

Several years ago Rhonda and John Smit were living in Kalamazoo and looking for a way to change their lives. "We wanted to move to northern Michigan and do something to cater to people who have interests similar to ours," remembers Rhonda. "We also dreamed of building a log home. So we put the two together and created a place for people who like the serenity of the woods and water and all that goes along with it."

And their business plan? Rhonda laughs and says, "We wrote it on a paper plate while we were camping!" They bought thirty spectacular acres along the west branch of the Sturgeon River in 1995 and broke ground for the B&B a year later.

What are "silent" sports?, I ask. "No motors!"

It's always fun to see a B&B that has been created specifically for that purpose from the ground up. Rhonda and John designed their three-level home to have four guest rooms—two on the lower level and two on the second floor, each with a private bath. There is a common room on each level, too. On the second floor, it's a loft that is open to the large living room below. On the lower level, it opens to the woods and gardens. The setup offers guests lots of privacy, and it's perfect for couples traveling together or families that take both rooms on one floor. The

dining room was built as a porch, but it is now enclosed with windows on three sides, and it has a heated floor so you can eat breakfast there year round and observe all the goings on outside.

The décor here is warm and up-north lodgy! The king- and queen-size beds are one-of-a-kind works of art, handcrafted from logs, and they're covered with quilts. Each room reflects the natural resources in northern Michigan that Rhonda and John love so much—woods and water, meadows and Michigan "mountains." The Cedar Room has a two-person whirlpool tub, and the River Room has a private balcony, which overlooks the woods and garden pond.

John grooms three miles of trails on the land for hiking and cross-country skiing. Skis can be rented nearby if you don't have your own, and you can borrow snowshoes at the lodge. Rhonda says she and John love snowshoeing, and they like to introduce their guests to it. In fact they hold a special snowshoe-making weekend, which includes two nights' lodging, breakfast and lunch on Saturday, breakfast on Sunday, and a kit so you can make your own snowshoes with guided instruction from John. The lessons usually begin Friday evening, and by Saturday afternoon, you'll be ready to start trekking!

Kayaking is big in this area. If you don't have your own, you can rent

from several outfitters who will transport you to a spot upriver on the main branch of the Sturgeon.

The Sturgeon River has been declared a blue ribbon trout stream by the State of Michigan, and the west branch of the river flows just a few hundred feet from the lodge. It's cold, clean and clear—exactly what trout require. To be certified, the state looks for "excellence": excellent water quality, excellent stocks of wild resident trout, the physical characteristics to permit fly casting but shallow enough to wade, diverse insect life and good fly hatches, and an earned reputation for providing an excellent trout-fishing experience.

Another aspect of the lodge that guests love is that it is less than an hour's drive from Petoskey, Boyne City, and the Mackinac Bridge, so it's a great destination for couples who have different interests. If one likes to fish and the other hikes or wants to shop or relax in the garden, they can go their separate ways. "When we have groups of couples, sometimes the men go in one direction and the women go in another," says Rhonda.

Spring holds special fun when the Smits tap their maple trees and make syrup. A maple syrup weekend offers guests the opportunity to help gather sap and watch it turn into syrup in the wood-fired evapora-

Rhonda's nontoxic cleaners

All-Purpose Cleaner

1/4 cup white vinegar
2 teaspoons borax
3 1/2 cups hot water
10 drops lemon essential oil
10 drops lavender essential oil
1/4 cup liquid dish soap

In a 32-ounce spray bottle, mix thoroughly the vinegar, borax and water. Add essential oils. Add dish soap last. Shake

Laundry Detergent

1 bar Fels-Naptha soap finely grated
1 cup washing soda
1 cup borax

Mix and store in an airtight container. Use 1 tablespoon per load of laundry or 2 tablespoons for heavily soiled laundry in warm or cold water.

---

tor. Each guest that weekend goes home with a small bottle of syrup as a tasty reminder of their efforts.

Rhonda and John both have a hand in making breakfast, and they use as many seasonal, organic and locally grown or raised ingredients as possible. The eggs come from their free-ranging hens, and they have a greenhouse and garden that yield bushels of vegetables. When we talked in late September, Rhonda was serving pumpkin-spiced pancakes with apple cider syrup. Heirloom tomatoes, not often thought of as a breakfast food, are a big hit with guests here. Rhonda serves them sliced with olive oil and basil and says they are a perfect side to egg dishes. John makes a great fruit salad.

Silent Sport Lodge has won recognition for its ecofriendly, energy-efficient practices, and it holds a Green Lodge certification from the State of Michigan. The home is heated with water from an outdoor, wood-fired boiler, and the wood it burns is a by-product of the hardwood flooring industry. Light bulbs are low-wattage compact fluorescent lamps. The Smits reuse and recycle. Appliances are Energy Star rated, and Rhonda makes most of their nontoxic cleaning products using ingredients such as vinegar, borax and washing soda. Their stewardship of the land is an admirable and responsible pursuit, and it fits seamlessly with Rhonda and John's love of the out of doors and their enjoyment in sharing it with others.

If you'd like to settle into the area for several days, ask the Smits about their two-bedroom, one-bath River Cabin one mile from the lodge. It sits just 75 feet from the river—so close you can hear it. They also offer a one-bedroom River Cottage on the main branch of the Sturgeon River, 2 miles south of Wolverine and a quarter mile from the North Central State Trail. Both have fully equipped kitchens.

Vitals

rooms: 4 with private baths, plus a 2-bedroom cabin and 1-bedroom cottage

pets permitted: no

pets in residence: one outdoor cat

open season: year-round

rates: $100 to $175

e-mail: silentsportlodge@att.net

website: www.silentsportlodge.com

owners/innkeepers:
Rhonda and John Smit
14750 Old Sturgeon Road
Wolverine, MI 49799
231-525-6166

SOUTHERN SUNSET: THE SOUTHWESTERN LOWER PENINSULA

Allegan
Castle in the Country

Grand Haven
Harbor House Inn

Holland
Crimson Cottage in the Woods

Muskegon
Port City Victorian Inn

St. Joseph
South Cliff Inn

Saugatuck
Belvedere Inn
Wickwood Inn

South Haven
Yelton Manor Bed and Breakfast

Whitehall
A Finch Nest Bed and Breakfast
Cocoa Cottage Bed and Breakfast
White Swan Inn

ALLEGAN

Castle in the Country

Once upon a time, in a kingdom south of Allegan, John and Caroline Wurtz built a marvelous three-story summer home that everyone for miles around called the Castle. The 1906 Queen Anne beauty had welcoming wraparound porches and a genuine turret where a beautiful princess could have awaited the return of her beloved prince.

By 1990, castles having fallen temporarily out of favor, it had broken windows, resident squirrels and a flooded basement. Ruth and Herb Boven saw beyond all that to the still intact quarter-sawn oak woodwork and big rooms, which were perfect for the bed-and-breakfast inn they wanted to create. And this is where the real-life fairy tale begins. Working side by side with two very young children in tow, they brought the home back to its former state of grace in just a year and a half and opened for guests in 1992.

Ruth is the seventh of eight children, so she was used to a full house, and she loved it. She dissolved her consulting business and ran the inn full time. Five years later, recognizing that the bed-and-breakfast market was changing and their children were growing, the Bovens added private baths and whirlpool tubs to several of the guest rooms and an addition for their own living quarters.

The inn prospered, and Herb left his full-time work to help manage it. Then came an innkeeper's dream. The adjacent 60 acres that were original to their castle came up for sale. The land included an enchanted forest, rolling meadows, a pond and lake frontage, plus an artistic 8,700-square-foot home built in the 1980s with big rooms that had been designed for . . . bed-and-breakfast lodging.

"It was really miraculous!" says Ruth. They bought it and opened the Castle Keep, with five guest rooms, more contemporary than vintage, and each with a private bath and whirlpool tub. The rooms are, without exception, lovely. I was delighted by the whimsical Romeo

and Juliet Suite with its tiny inside balcony overlooking the sleeping area, and I felt an instant sense of calm in the Keep's first-floor Camelot Suite. It is barrier free and has wall-mounted crystal fireplaces in both the sleeping room and the lavish bathroom.

The Keep sits deep in the property, about 300 yards from the Castle. It houses the inn's kitchen and dining room where all the guests gather for breakfast. And it offers great rest and recreational opportunities for guests of both the Castle and the Keep. There are outdoor bistro tables and sitting areas around an outdoor fireplace, a gazebo at the edge of the pond, trails through the woods to a screen house at the lake, and kayaks and a paddle boat for guests' use.

The Bovens wanted the inn to be the perfect destination for couples wanting a romantic getaway, so they added options such as picnic lunches and dinners for two, and they furnished the large lower level of the Keep for spa services so you can pamper every inch of your body from your toes up! One room has two massage tables so both members of a couple can get the royal treatment at the same time.

I asked if guests staying in the Castle mind going to the Keep for breakfast. Ruth said it's quite the opposite. They enjoy the quiet walk down the little country lane and frequently get to see deer, hawks and eagles. And in the winter?

"They love it!" Ruth laughed. "Sometimes they stop and make

The castle keep

In days of old when knights were bold, the fortified part of a castle was called the keep. It was often a tower, and it was used as a place of last refuge if the castle came under attack. The soldiers were sometimes garrisoned there, and the king and queen were brought to the keep if they needed extra protection.

snowmen and snow angels along the way!" If you'd rather stay cozy in bed, you can add a package that includes the option of breakfast delivered to your room. Wherever you choose to eat breakfast, don't miss it! Herb is the cook, and he makes everything from scratch. His cream scones and pub pies are becoming legendary. You'll find several of his favorite recipes on the Castle Kingdom blog.

While there is certainly a "castlelike" feeling here, it is subtle, elegant and blended artfully with contemporary luxury. Even in the Victorian era Castle, the furnishings are sleek, and there are just enough antique touches and original architectural features to remind you that you're in a turn-of-the-century home. Both buildings have central air-conditioning, and each guest room has a fireplace—electric, gas, crystal or one of the home's original wood-burning hearths. What feels more romantic and cozy on a cold winter night, or even a cool summer morning, than a fireplace?

If you're ready to relax, go to the inn's website and look at the options and packages you can add to a night or two of lodging. Ruth can arrange for all kinds of activities to carry you through the day, from breakfast in bed to a chocolate oil massage. And if you just want to add a few goodies to celebrate something special, ask about flowers, candies and even special cakes.

Vitals

rooms: 10 with private baths

pets: no

pets in residence: a poodle, which is not allowed in guests' quarters, and an outdoor cat.

rates: $139 to $339

open season: year-round

e-mail: info@castleinthecountry.com

website: www.castleinthecountry.com

owners/innkeepers:
Ruth and Herb Boven
340 M-40 South
Allegan, MI 49010
269-673-8054
888-673-8054

GRAND HAVEN

Harbor House Inn

This distinctive pink-shuttered inn looks as though it has been here for ages, but in fact it was built in 1987 in a classic Victorian cottage style that gives guests the warmth and homeyness of a vintage lodging with modern conveniences. It's also a bit of a hybrid—a cross between a small hotel and a large bed and breakfast. Perched above the street overlooking Grand Haven's waterfront, it offers guests a bird's-eye view of the busy channel running from Lake Michigan to Spring Lake with its parade of watercraft in the summer, and it is perfectly situated for exploring this pretty lakeside town on foot. From the inn, it's an easy stroll along the boardwalk to the lighthouse, Grand Haven State Park, sandy beaches, shops and restaurants. For old-fashioned summer relaxation, you'll love the wicker-filled screened porch. If the weather becomes inclement (in Michigan?) and you decide to stay inside, there's a bright living room on the first floor, which you'll see when you check in, and an adjacent library with board games, books and DVDs. Both rooms have fireplaces and are wonderfully cozy when the wind is howling off the lake.

The inn's fifteen sleeping rooms are decorated individually in a blend of reproduction Victorian and country cottage styles, and most have a full or partial view of the harbor. Each comes equipped with a telephone, hair dryer, ironing board and iron, TV and DVD player, and they are individually air-conditioned. The beds are king or queen size, and most of the king beds can be converted to twins with some advanced notice. For a little extra indulgence, reserve one of the Premium Rooms with a fireplace and whirlpool tub. That almost guarantees a memorable stay even if it rains all day and the fish don't bite.

A breakfast buffet is offered every morning from 8:00 to 10:00 a.m. and includes homemade coffee cakes, fresh fruit, the inn's custom cereal blend, a selection of cheeses, a fragrant cinnamon bread, yogurt and hard-boiled eggs. From 6:00 to 9:00 p.m., you'll find additional tasty

offerings—a selection of sweets such as brownies or cookies and beverages. And if you wonder about the wonderful aroma wafting out of the kitchen after breakfast, it's probably another batch of the inn's signature caramels, which the staff makes daily. You'll find them by your bedside each evening.

Adjacent to the Harbor House is the Harbor Cottage, which accommodates guests in two spacious suites that can be rented separately or together. One of the two, the Garden Suite, includes a galley kitchen with a refrigerator, microwave, coffeemaker and dishes. The inn's newest addition is the Captain's Cottage just to the east. It has three suites, each with a bedroom, galley kitchen, living room with a fireplace, private bath and private outdoor sitting area. Guests staying in the cottages are invited to enjoy the buffet breakfast and evening treats in the inn as well.

Grand Haven is a hub of activity in summer. Its famous US Coast Guard Festival draws thousands for a week of activities, and the synchronized performances of music and water at the Musical Fountain, just across the channel from the inn, have been a nightly summer tradition since 1962. Charter fishing boats leave daily from the docks a few blocks away. For a little whimsical summer fun and a tour of the town, catch the Harbor Trolley, which operates from 11:00 a.m. to 10:00 p.m.

seven days a week, Memorial Day thru Labor Day. It makes scheduled pickups at Chinook Pier, the State Park, The Bookman bookstore and Pfaff Pharmacy, and you can flag it down to be picked up anywhere along the route. The pristine beach in Grand Haven has been voted among the best in the country, and if you're a bicyclist, you'll love the 100 miles of bicycle trails in the area.

A winter vacation at the lakeshore can be pretty wonderful. There are excellent cross-country ski areas nearby and good ice fishing during the darkest cold days. Thirty years ago I remember that most of the little shops in cities and villages along the lake closed after the "color" season, and traffic lights went from stop and go to blinking until the tourists began to return in the spring. These days, with the variety of popular winter sports, cities like Grand Haven no longer roll up the sidewalks in the fall. In fact, in the past few years, Grand Haven has installed *heated* sidewalks throughout downtown!

Vitals

rooms: 15 in the inn, 5 suites in the 2 cottages

pets: no

pets in residence: none

open season: year-round, closed Thanksgiving Day, Christmas Eve and Christmas Day

rates: $99 to $280

e-mail: innkeeper@harborhousegh.com

website: www.harborhousegh.com

innkeeper:
Linda Rosema
114 South Harbor Drive
Grand Haven, MI 49417
616-846-0610
800-841-0610

HOLLAND

Crimson Cottage in the Woods

What a wonderful surprise it was to find this lovely bed and breakfast! Crimson Cottage is tucked in a wooded dune at the end of a private drive, and it's cozy as can be. Owners Kathy and Michael Henry built it and opened for business in 2007, but the idea had been hatching for years.

"When we got married, we stayed in a B&B in Northport," remembers Kathy. "We loved it, and it was always in the back of my mind that this was what I wanted to do." But retirement, or at least semiretirement, had to come first.

After many years of planning, they created a home with a contemporary cottage look that is both elegant and casual. It's just 1½ miles from Lake Michigan and 10 minutes by car to downtown Holland. But it's so comfortable you might decide you'd rather stay put and relax on the dune garden patio overlooking Mallard Pond, linger over coffee in the sun-room or take a walk on the nearby bike path.

Kathy worked in hospital administration, and Michael is a clinical psychologist. They understand stress, and they've created a home that is perfect for destressing. The first floor is given over to a welcoming gathering room with a fabulous red and white checked couch and comfy chairs in front of a fireplace, an open dining area and a huge open kitchen. The space is tranquil and filled with natural light, and it flows together beautifully. I love the fact that you can pull up a chair and talk to Kathy while she's making breakfast. She likes that, too!

Guest rooms are located on the second floor, and each is fresh and colorful. Just Beachy is decorated in white and blueberry blue. The Crimson Cottage Suite has shades of pale yellow with red accents. Moku Lani, meaning "Island Heaven," has a sophisticated tropical motif inspired by the Henrys' love of Hawaii, plus a large corner gas

fireplace and a table and chairs for two. Each room has a king-size bed, a private bath and convenient extras such as a coffeemaker, refrigerator, filtered water, TV and DVD player and plush robes. Moku Lani also has a large built-in jetted tub and a separate shower.

Alice's Garden is named for Kathy's mother. She was a fine artist, and several of her paintings grace the walls of this peaceful room. It's available by special arrangement.

Breakfast includes hot entrées such as baked French toast, egg casseroles, granola, pastries and fruit. Depending on the number of guests, it can be set up as a buffet on the stunning granite island or served in the sun-room, which overlooks the pond. If you happen to get hungry or thirsty early in the morning or late in the evening—or even in the middle of the night—you'll find a hospitality table on the second floor with hot beverages and Kathy's signature chocolate chip cookies.

Holland is a fun place to explore, and there are four seasons of activities to bring you here. The Tulip Festival in the spring is spectacular. Driving through the town when millions of carefully planted and tended tulips are in bloom is a sight that defies description. The city owes the idea to biology teacher Lida Rogers, who suggested in 1927, at a Woman's Literary Club meeting, that Holland adopt the tulip as its flower and set aside a day for a festival. In 1928 the city purchased one

Tulipomania

Most of us associate tulips with the Netherlands, but they are not native to that tiny country. As early as AD 1000, the Turks were cultivating tulips from the mountainous region of Central Asia that borders Russia and China. Botanist Carolus Clusius discovered tulips growing in Vienna in 1593 and began cultivating them in the Netherlands. They quickly showed their potential when some of Clusius's collection was stolen and cultivated.

Within a few years, the tulip became a prized possession that only the very wealthy could afford, setting off a frenzy in 1634 referred to as Tulipomania. Historians believe it reached the height of its craziness in early February 1637. Guardians of an orphanage in the Dutch village of Alkmaar had received a valuable collection of tulip bulbs, and they decided to auction them to generate support for some of the children.

The auction opened early on February 5. Single bulbs began selling for as much as 200 guilders apiece. By comparison, a carpenter at that time could expect *annual earnings* of about 250 guilders. As the auction progressed, prices rose. Single bulbs went for 400 guilders, 600 guilders and then 1,000 guilders—about one-third the annual earnings of a well-to-do merchant. By the end of the day, roughly 90,000 guilders had been taken in for the orphanage—a huge fortune!

The New York office of the Associated Bulb Growers of Holland lists the following as a record for the price of *one single tulip bulb* during Tulipomania: a load of grain, 4 oxen, 12 sheep, 5 pigs, 2 tubs of butter, 1,000 pounds of cheese, 4 barrels of beer, 2 hogsheads of wine, a suit of clothes and a silver drinking cup.

By the end of 1637, the tulip market had crashed. They were, after all, only humble little bulbs, which, when planted, produce pretty flowers.

Despite this rocky start and the ruin of many family fortunes, the Dutch remain devoted to the tulip. The Netherlands produces about three billion tulip bulbs each year and exports two billion of them. The United States is the top importer of tulip bulbs.

[My thanks go to the Holland Area Convention and Visitors Bureau and Mike Dash, the author of *Tulipomania, The Story of the World's Most Coveted Flower and the Extraordinary Passions It Aroused.*]

hundred thousand tulip bulbs from the Netherlands and planted them. Bulbs were also sold to Holland residents for a penny each. The following spring tulips bloomed throughout the city, and Holland invited visitors to come and enjoy their beauty during a week in May. With the addition of early- and late-flowering tulips, the city is now abloom for weeks. Do put Tulip Time on your bucket list.

Summer brings festivals, beach days, art gallery walks, concerts and street performers. Fall's crisp days invite long bike rides and color tours. And winter . . . well, for starters, the sidewalks downtown are heated and ice free, so shop on! There are also great cross-country ski trails nearby. Hope College offers year-round cultural events, and Kathy and Michael can direct you to brewpubs, bistros and romantic waterfront restaurants. Saugatuck and Douglas are roughly twenty minutes away by car in one direction. Grand Haven is twenty minutes in the other direction.

The inn has three bicycles for your use. For a little special pampering, ask about scheduling an in-room massage. If you're staying in Moku Lani, you can schedule massages for two.

Vitals

> *rooms:* 3 with private baths and a 4th available by special arrangement

pets permitted: no

pets in residence: none

open season: year-round

rates: $130 to $189

e-mail: kathy@crimsoncottageinn.com

website: www.crimsoncottageinn.com

owners/innkeepers:
Kathy and Michael Henry
2009 West Lakewood Blvd.
Holland, MI 49424
616-994-0922

MUSKEGON

Port City Victorian Inn

Alexander Rodgers Sr. made his way from Scotland to Maine, then traveled to Muskegon by oxen and settled there in 1858. He was a skilled mechanic and machinist, and he opened the Rodgers Iron Manufacturing Company. It was the era of logging in Michigan, and Rodgers's company made thousands of hammers used in the industry, along with the "tooth bar log turner," which Alexander invented, and the Muskegon Spike Roller Edger. In 1868 the company was reorganized as the Muskegon Iron Works, with Alexander's four sons as stockholders. A year later Muskegon became a city, and Alexander Rodgers became one of its first officials.

Alexander's business endeavors blossomed, and his fortune grew. He sat on many influential boards of directors and invested in up-and-coming enterprises such as the Temperance Reform Opera House. He also built a lumber mill on the south side of Muskegon Lake, which produced more than 32 million board feet in 1875.

That same year he built a spectacular Queen Anne home on the southeastern bluff of the lake where he owned hundreds of acres. It was a grand example of the Victorian style, complete with curved glass windows and much gingerbread—a fine tribute to his success. He lived in the home until 1914.

Barbara and Fred Schossau had never dreamed of operating an inn until they discovered this beauty in 1993. They toured it and returned to see it a second time. One of its previous owners, Josephine Cutshall, had lived there for fifty years, hoping to keep it from being torn down and replaced with modern buildings, as was the fate of other mansions in the neighborhood. By the time Barb and Fred saw it, it had been for sale for two and a half years.

"The trees and gardens around the house were all overgrown," remembers Fred. "We could barely see it from the road, and everything

needed fixing—plumbing, electrical, the boiler, the roof, dozens of windows . . . but the foundation was solid and the woodwork was in good shape." And, oh yes, the realtor mentioned that it would make a nice bed and breakfast . . .

They bought the house in August and opened the following spring when the first room, the Queen Anne, was ready. It took a few years to finish the other four guest rooms, and I can tell you, they were worth the wait.

Each room is decorated around a theme or family name and furnished with fine antiques and accessories, lovely linens and reproduction English Victorian wall coverings. Everywhere you look, you'll see examples of Barb and Fred's attention to detail. The luxurious Queen Anne Room has a vintage queen-size oak bed and tall oak armoire, and through its 5 foot by 7 foot front window you get a great view of Muskegon Lake and the lakeshore's spectacular sunsets. The ceiling fan is a replica of an 1860s Hunter design, and there are three sweet sconces that were added to the room when it was converted from gas lighting to electric. The attached private bath has a whirlpool tub and heat lamps for extra comfort.

The Captain's Cabin Suite is a favorite of guests celebrating special occasions. It's a large, handsome room with a stately queen-size bed, a two-person Jacuzzi waterfall tub, a replica of a coal-burning fireplace and a comfy sitting room. French doors lead to a private balcony with a view of Muskegon Lake. There is also a table for two, and you're welcome to have breakfast there.

For a softer choice, consider the Alexander Rodgers Room. I love its tall four-poster bed draped with yards of chiffon. The Rose Room has an equally dreamy tulle-draped queen-size sleigh bed and a petite sitting area with a gas fireplace. The large attached bath is original, installed in 1911. Anastasia's Room has a striking black walnut East Lake bedroom set and overlooks the grassy park next door. All the guest rooms have high-definition TV, DVDs and DVD players.

At the end of the hall on the second floor you can step outside to the Victorian-inspired, pergola-covered porch, which Fred designed and built. It's a popular spot in the summer. Barb hung curtains around one area so guests who arrange for a pampering package can opt to have a massage in a private space on the porch in warm weather instead of in their rooms.

There are many original features that stand out in this house, and you'll notice them from the moment you walk in. The builder used abundant buttery oak for the floors and ash for window trim, beveled-glass pocket doors and a hand-carved stairway. The leaded, curved glass in the front bay window is rare and beautiful. Several common areas

give you plenty of options for gathering with other guests or finding a quiet corner to yourself. The front parlor on the first floor has a splendid view of Muskegon Lake and the Lakeshore Yacht Harbor. From there you can walk through the spacious dining room and into the fireplace parlor. The south-facing sun-room is flooded with light from its fourteen windows. There is another sitting area on the second floor with a view of the lake. The windows throughout the inn are large and draped with miles of lace, which lets in lots of natural light.

Throughout the renovation, Barb and Fred installed features to make the mansion more "green." The boiler, for example, is a Viessmann design from Germany, which is extremely efficient and heats the tap water as well as water for the heating system. Each room has a remote-controlled, state-of-the-art air-conditioning system, too. Also rare for a Victorian house . . . it's entirely insulated!

Barb is the breakfast cook, and Fred says guests love her made-from-scratch buttermilk pancakes and peach cake. She also makes tasty quiches and other hot dishes, and there are always baked goods and fruit cups with Barb's special toppings. She serves breakfast at 9:00 a.m. unless guests request another time. She's happy to accommodate business travelers who need to eat earlier and guests taking the Cross Lake Ferry.

Some of the home's original decorative exterior trimmings were removed in the last century, and the fancy Queen Anne exterior was toned down a bit when sleeker lines became popular. Yet the elegance remains, and while you're having breakfast in this lovely setting, it's easy to imagine the gracious lifestyle that Mr. Rodgers and his family enjoyed. Do ask to see old photos of the house. They date back to its earliest days when the sidewalks were wooden and ladies' dresses swept the ground.

From the inn, it's a short drive to Lake Michigan beaches, Michigan's Adventure amusement park and two state parks. Muskegon's L.C. Walker Arena is home to the city's professional hockey team. Local theaters feature music and theatrical productions through the year. If you're a fan of maritime history, head to the USS *Silversides* Submarine Museum adjacent to the Muskegon Channel. For winter activity, try the lighted luge, ice-skating rink and cross-country ski trails at Muskegon State Park's winter sports complex or fish through the ice for walleye and bluegill.

When you visit the inn's website you'll notice the sign of the fish, a long- established symbol that Christians use to express their faith. For Barb and Fred, it's recognition that the Port City Victorian Inn is a Christian-owned B&B. And while like-minded travelers often seek them out, they welcome people of all faiths. In fact one of the things they like best about being innkeepers is that they have hosted guests from every corner of the world and all backgrounds.

Vitals

rooms: 5 with private baths

pets permitted: no

pets in residence: yes, a sweet Yorkshire terrier

open season: year-round

rates: $150 to $225

e-mail: pcvicinn@comcast.net

website: www.portcityinn.com

owners/innkeepers:
Barbara and Frederick Schossau
1259 Lakeshore Drive
Muskegon, MI 49441
231-759-0205
800-274-3574

ST. JOSEPH

South Cliff Inn

Bill Swisher has the kind of varied background that's perfect for a successful innkeeper. He was raised on a farm and remembers standing on a chair cooking when he was five years old. He was an executive chef in a French restaurant. He sold cars. He taught school in Venezuela. And he did a lot of other things before he took two years off and traveled the country in an Airstream trailer. Then he went to the East Coast to visit bed and breakfasts and do some homework. When he came back to St. Joe, he opened South Cliff Inn.

As the name implies, this little inn sits on a cliff overlooking Lake Michigan. If you walk to the edge, you'll see Amtrak's rails running along the shore far below. There are two large decks from which you can watch the lake display its year-round beauty. If cold weather drives you inside, you can curl up in front of the fireplace in the living room where there's often soft background music playing. Bill designed the inn to have a sense of both elegance and take-your-shoes-off comfort, and there's not a hint of stuffiness here.

Imported and designer fabrics have been handpicked for each of the seven guest rooms. In fact, among his many skills, Bill is amazingly handy with a sewing machine, and he made many of the beautiful curtains and bedcovers. The rooms vary greatly in size from the petite and bright Morning Room on the first floor, just off the entrance, to the Study on the second floor. This warm, welcoming suite has a balcony overlooking Lake Michigan, a whirlpool tub in the bedroom and a gas fireplace. The first-floor Harbor Room has a whirlpool tub in the bedroom as well, and the tub is surrounded on two sides with windows that offer a view of the lake. On the lower level is the two-room Admiral Suite, which is reached by a private outside entrance. It has a bedroom plus a large sitting room with a fireplace. All the guest rooms have flat-screen TVs. Many are tucked out of sight in armoires.

I love the great variety of guest rooms here, because it means you can choose the features you want—from a lovely no-frills room that is very affordable to one that is luxuriously indulgent.

Breakfast is served buffet style, and you're in for a treat. On a recent visit, I sat in the living room polishing off a slice of wonderfully rich cream cheese coffee cake that Bill had made that morning and was reminded how much he loves to cook for his guests. He even published a cookbook several years ago, and some of his return guests request their favorite dishes from his vast files going back to when he opened the inn in 1987! Your morning repast will likely include frittatas or other egg dishes, pastries, breads, fruit and beverages. Bread pudding, one of my all-time favorites, is a staple every morning as well. When possible, Bill uses ingredients that are locally raised and grown. "I have a little saying," he says with a chuckle. "The lake brings them here, but the food brings them back!"

Guests are welcome to eat outdoors when weather permits or in one of two indoor dining areas, including a sun-room that faces the lake. Besides the fine view, you'll get a look at another of Bill's skills. He is an accomplished stained-glass artist, and panels of his work hang in the windows. He also made the stained-glass windows in the living room, which mirror the 1920s–1930s style of the home so well that I assumed they were original. The gorgeous stained-glass lampshade in the living room is his creation, too.

Bill speaks with enthusiasm about St. Joseph. "It's such a great town!," he says, as he begins to tell me all there is to do nearby. He can head you in the direction of antique shops and wineries, if those are

Bill's breakfast casserole

12 to 14 slices of cheap white bread, crusts cut off
2 packages frozen chopped spinach, thawed and squeezed dry
1 13-ounce can of sliced mushrooms, drained
2 cups grated sharp cheddar cheese
3 cups shredded Italian blend cheese
8 eggs or 2 cups of an egg product
2 cups milk
3 tablespoons prepared mustard
3 teaspoons granulated garlic
1 teaspoon ground pepper
1 teaspoon salt

Spray a 9 by 13 baking pan. Butter the bread on one side. Place
    7 slices buttered side down in the pan.
Layer half the spinach and half the mushrooms over the bread.
Cover with the Italian blend cheese.
Place the rest of the slices of bread on top, buttered side up.
Top with remaining spinach and mushrooms and the cheddar
    cheese.
Beat together the eggs, milk and seasonings and pour evenly
    over everything so it's covered.
Refrigerater overnight.
Bake in a 350° oven the next morning for 45 minutes to 1 hour.
While it's baking, mix together:

1 10 3/4--ounce can of mushroom soup
1 1/2 cups sour cream
1 cup grated sharp cheddar cheese
1 7-ounce can of sliced mushrooms, drained

Pour the ingredients over the casserole and bake for another 35
    to 45 minutes. Let it stand for 15 minutes before serving.

Note: you can substitute ham or roasted chicken for the spinach
and mushrooms. You can also substitute 3/4 cup chopped roasted peppers and 2 cups of sautéed onions for the mushrooms.

your preference, or to U-pick fruit and vegetable farms if you want to
sample local produce. Downtown St. Joseph has sweet shops, and it's
very walkable. If you like music and the arts, time your visit to coincide with community theater presentations and free outdoor concerts.
The four public beaches on Lake Michigan are a worthy destination in

themselves, and you can't beat the dramatic beauty of Lake Michigan at sunset. If you want to fish, you can reserve a place on a charter boat that departs from the St. Joseph harbor. There's also a Jack Nicklaus Signature Design golf course just minutes away.

Amtrak stops in St. Joe. If South Cliff Inn is your destination and you're coming by train, let Bill know when you make your reservation, and he will pick you up at the station.

Vitals

rooms: 7 with private baths

pets permitted: no

pets in residence: none

open season: year-round

rates: $85 to $259

e-mail: InnInformation@SouthCliffInn.com

website: www.southcliffinn.com

owner/innkeeper:
Bill Swisher
1900 Lakeshore Drive
St. Joseph, MI 49085
269-983-4881

SAUGATUCK

Belvedere Inn

To paraphrase the Belvedere Inn's website, *you need no passport here, and there are no additional baggage charges, but it's a world away.*

First, a bit of background on this extraordinary inn. In 1897 members of the Comstock family of Chicago purchased a large plot of land in the countryside a few miles from Saugatuck. They built an elegant wood-frame home there with several outbuildings and cultivated a farm that supplied Chicago markets with a variety of fruits and berries. In 1912 Mr. and Mrs. John D. Williamson purchased the estate, and less than six weeks later they stood by helplessly and watched their beautiful home burn to the ground after it was hit by lightning. When they made plans to rebuild, Mr. Williamson declared that their new residence would be fireproof. Their grand prairie-style home was designed by Frank Lloyd Wright's colleague Dwight Perkins, who specified 12-inch-thick masonry walls for safety and stylish details such as quarter-sawn oak trim. From their hilltop paradise, the Williamsons could see Lake Michigan and the sand dunes. *Belvedere* is Italian for "beautiful view."

A large water tower was added to the property, along with a hip-roof barn, which is now Saugatuck's Red Barn Summer Playhouse. Eight years later Mr. Williamson traded the home in a real estate transaction, and for the next several decades, it went through a succession of owners. It caught the eye of John Lottie, who purchased it in 1995 and began a masterful renovation to turn the home into an inn. He was even able to reinstall several original features, such as French doors and light fixtures, removed by earlier owners and found!

Shaun Glynn and Pete Ta acquired the Belvedere in 2003, giving the inn and its guests the benefit of their passion for entertaining and their more than twenty-five years of hospitality and business experience. Ten lodging rooms occupy the second and third floors, and all have been redecorated in a sophisticated style that will remind you of fine Euro-

pean boutique hotels. A fireplace was added to each room, and jetted tubs were added to three suites. Guests have the use of a delightful sun-room and a library with books, games and a large movie collection. A wraparound veranda overlooks the inn's gardens where you'll find a quiet pond and places to sit, and you can enjoy that feeling of being a world away. You'll also be well fed. Your day will begin with a full breakfast, and in both the afternoon and evening, you'll be offered fresh-from-the-kitchen sweets and beverages.

The Belvedere Restaurant occupies the first floor of the inn and is overseen by Shaun, a talented and delightful chef who hails from Galway, Ireland, and was trained in European schools and restaurants. Shaun describes his offerings as Old World classic continental dishes, and he puts an emphasis on using seasonal and local ingredients. One of the most popular items served is chateaubriand for two. "The decadent béarnaise that we make to order for each guest melts in your mouth!," says Shaun. And it's served with the inn's famous scalloped cream potatoes. Other guests' favorites include roasted butternut squash and crabmeat bisque and the inn's lovely signature dish of mussels in Pernod cream.

If you haven't time to spend the night, do stop for dinner. The menu is a la carte and prix fixe depending on whether you want to have two, three or four courses. Ask about the highly popular bed-and-breakfast and dinner package ("come for dinner and stay for breakfast!") available midweek in the summer and weekends in the off-season. With two consecutive lodging nights, you get a $100 dining certificate, which is the cost of the Belvedere's four-course dinner for two. Yes, you read that right. The certificate covers the cost of your dinner. Four courses. It's an amazing offer.

If you want to have wine with your dinner, you'll find a large selection to choose from, and if you really want to have fun, consider attending a wine-pairing dinner. Shaun and Pete hold several throughout the year. And ask about joining their wine club.

Everything from the fine linens to the well-tended gardens, the expertly prepared food and excellent service at the Belvedere are meant to wrap you in comfortable elegance and make you feel welcome. If you're looking for extra pampering, ask about amenities you can reserve with your room, such as a bottle of wine, therapeutic massage and chocolate-dipped strawberries. Even looking at the website is a nice experience—the hauntingly beautiful music from *Phantom of the Opera* plays in the background.

Because of the grand spaces and lovely outdoor areas, the Belvedere is well suited for hosting celebrations of all kinds, from corporate retreats to weddings and outdoor tented events for up to 350 people.

The Belvedere is located on a picturesque country road just a few

minutes by car from downtown Saugatuck, Douglas and Lake Michigan. Holland is just to the north, with its Dutch village, Tulip Festival and heated sidewalks in the winter. All summer long, there are fairs and festivals along the lakeshore. Summer theater is produced across the street in the Belvedere's original barn. Golf, cross-country skiing and antique markets are nearby. The staff at the inn will help you with ideas and directions.

If you're looking for long-term vacation accommodations, ask about the lovely Bellevue Harbor House that Shaun and Pete have also created. It's a home on Saugatuck's waterfront that will accommodate eight people and is available by the week.

Vitals

rooms: 10 rooms and suites, all with private baths

pets permitted: no

pets in residence: none

open season: The inn is open year-round. The restaurant is open Tuesday through Sunday, May through October, and on weekends during the off-season. Seating time is 6:00 p.m., with an additional seating at 8:00 during summer weekends and selected other months. Call or check the website to get details and make reservations.

rates: $135 to $345 double occupancy. Dinner per person is $40 for two courses, $45 for three courses and $50 for four courses.

e-mail: info@thebelvedereinn.com

website: www.thebelvedereinn.com

owners/innkeepers:
Shaun Glynn and Pete Ta
3656 63rd Street
Saugatuck, MI 49453
269-857-5777
877-858-5777

SAUGATUCK

Wickwood Inn

It was a sultry summer day when I last visited the Wickwood Inn, and the picturesque village of Saugatuck was bustling. Inside the inn, all was cool, calm and inviting. There are so many things I love about Wickwood, and at the top of the list is this: the inn simply draws you in and invites you to be comfortable—to rest or read, to enjoy a glass of wine or a cup of coffee, to chat with friends, to cozy up next to the fireplace in the living room when a cold wind blows off Lake Michigan, to relax in the library. And then there are the wonderful aromas coming from the kitchen . . .

Owner Julee Rosso greeted me with her ever-present enthusiasm and a plate of fresh-baked cookies, a special treat from the woman who cofounded the famed Silver Palate gourmet take-out shop in New York City and wrote five best-selling Silver Palate cookbooks, including one that is in the Cookbook Hall of Fame.

Julee and her husband, Bill Miller, bought the inn in 1991 and filled it with things they love—French and English antiques, oriental rugs, designer fabrics and luxurious linens, fresh flowers, good books, comfortable overstuffed chairs and wonderful art. Oh, the art! Julee says the walls of their home are full, so the inn has become a showcase for their collection of paintings, prints and sculpture. It's part of the style of Wickwood, and each piece has a story. The enormous poster from France on the wall in the Toy Room, for example, hung for years in Julee's office in New York. She acquired the bigger than wall-size antique tapestry in the dining room while she was in Florence, Italy. Many of the paintings and sculptures were purchased from friends who are accomplished artists. For Julee, art is personal. "I bought a tiny Picasso plate in 1965," she laughs, "and we built a room around it!"

The eleven guest rooms are striking, thoroughly individual and,

like the Picasso Room, they began with a theme that has been carried
through in the linens and artwork, wall coverings and accessories. I love
the Matisse Room, decorated in classic country French blue and white,
with its framed Matisse *Cinquante Dessins* prints and a pretty white
and brass queen-size bed. The Lodge Suite, with its four-poster canopy
feather bed and two wingback chairs flanking the fireplace, feels every
bit like an Adirondack retreat. Each guest room room has a private bath
stocked with thick towels and bathrobes.

There is whimsy here, too. There's a vintage British telephone booth
in the hall outfitted with what has to be one of the last working pay
phones in the city!

If you're like me and a million other people, you have at least one
of Julee's great cookbooks in your kitchen. Luckily for guests at Wickwood, her time-tested recipes are standard fare. Luckily for all of us, she
posts favorite recipes in her website newsletter! So let me tell you about
food at Wickwood, because it is amazing.

It begins with candlelight hors d'oeuvres in the early evening—
artisanal cheese, roasted vegetables, shrimp and crab crostini, soups,
tarts and flatbreads, wine and juices and more. If you get hungry between
hors d'oeuvres and bedtime or bedtime and breakfast, you'll find a selection of sweets available around-the-clock to take off the edge.

Weekend breakfast is a champagne brunch with offerings such as
pecan sticky buns, a vegetable frittata, country ham, sugar and spice

For the love of food

Julee went to a dinner party in 1968 and dined on a stew that she thought was "out of this world!" Turns out it was made from a recipe in Julia Child's famous *Mastering the Art of French Cooking.* She bought the book and began working her way through it, trying recipe after recipe, and that, she says, was her introduction to fabulous food.

Several years later she was reading a book by a journalist who wrote of staying at an inn owned by two women from Provence, and he included several of their recipes. She was so inspired that she wanted to leave her job and go to work for them. "I'd chop carrots for them!," she laughs.

Instead, with partner Sheila Lukins, she opened The Silver Palate in New York, a tiny, remarkable take-out shop that quickly captured the hearts and stomachs of New Yorkers. It was a huge success, and Julee followed it with a line of Silver Palate foods and five cookbooks filled with stories about food and friends and the things she loves. She is credited with changing the way millions of us cook by showing us the pleasures of eating food in season, using fresh ingredients, keeping it simple and excellent and making it beautiful.

A recent trip to the South of France provided Julee some inspiration once again. She visited a little village where she learned that people in the early part of the last century traded rooms and food for art. And that got her thinking . . .

popovers, apple bread pudding and . . . oh my goodness . . . so much more. During the week, you'll find a newspaper and coffee or tea waiting for you, and a buffet that includes juices and fresh fruits, granola made at the inn and a selection of homemade muffins and sweet breads.

The dishes served change seasonally and from year to year. Julee purchases food that is grown or raised locally whenever possible, and on this summer morning, as she talked about her guests' favorite dishes— her cardamom cake is at the top of the list—she was enthused about a nearby organic berry farm. "We have a lot of repeat guests," she says, "and I always want to be doing the latest and greatest!"

Food here is more than just something to fill you up. It is a cause for celebration. When Julee describes in detail her summer squash frittata with goat cheese or the sticky buns with their delicate lemon glaze, you can tell she loves good food and, perhaps even more, loves serving good food to her guests.

Before I leave, Julee disappears and comes back with a napkin full of sweets. "Take these cookies with you!," she says with the warmest smile. I am delighted, and I plan to bring them home to share with Paul. I eat one before I get to the freeway. Or maybe two. I eat another before I reach Holland . . .

Vitals

rooms: 11 with private baths

pets permitted: no

pets in residence: none

open season: year-round

rates: $195 to $450

e-mail: innkeeper@wickwoodinn.com

website: www.wickwoodinn.com

owners/innkeepers:
Julee Rosso and Bill Miller
510 Butler Street
PO Box 1019
Saugatuck, MI 49453
269-857-1465
800-385-1174

SOUTH HAVEN

Yelton Manor Bed and Breakfast

When I first visited Yelton Manor Bed and Breakfast just a few years after it opened, gracious owner Elaine Herbert told me that everything in the inn was specifically designed with her guests in mind—luxury, elegance, comfort, pampering, privacy. And cookies! I loved her commitment to guests then, and I am delighted to say that the inn is even more wonderful and welcoming than it was when Elaine and her husband, Rob Kripaitis, first created this little piece of paradise across the street from Lake Michigan in 1988.

The two began this adventure by purchasing a many-gabled Victorian home that had been built in 1890 for the Delemere sisters, who ran it as a lakeside resort. When they took it over, Elaine and Rob embarked on a renovation of the entire structure, then decorated the rooms with beautiful linens and wall coverings and an elegant collection of reproduction and antique furnishings. They also added whirlpool tubs and gas fireplaces in several rooms for extra coziness.

Thinking about what guests love, Elaine wanted to add places for intimate out-of-your-room conversations and privacy, so she gathered wingback chairs and loveseats, small tables, good reading materials and reading lamps, and tucked them under those fine gables and into nooks on every floor of the inn. The result is that you'll feel at home here, whether you choose to socialize with others, find a sunny spot for two or curl up in a quiet corner away from the world with a favorite book and a glass of wine.

Just a few steps from the inn is the Yelton Manor Guest House. This slightly smaller sister mirrors the Manor's Victorian styling, with steep gables and a wraparound sun-room, and you'd never guess it was built in 1993. Each of its six guest rooms has both a fireplace and a whirlpool tub, and on each floor you'll find a small refrigerator for your use. The furnishings are similar to those in the Manor—romantic and sophisti-

cated. Paul and I stayed in the luxurious third-floor Dewey Hotel Suite in the Guest House—a perfect choice anytime, and especially if you're celebrating a special occasion. It has two intimate sitting areas and a tiny romantic balcony for two with a lake view.

In both the Manor and the Guest House, look for wonderful details like interior and exterior stained-glass windows, which let rainbows of light into sleeping rooms and baths, French doors, beautiful wall coverings, and a DVD player in each room. There is also an extensive collection of movies on DVD for guests' use. And don't worry about getting hungry here. You'll never be far from popcorn, a dish of candies, a plate of cookies, or Elaine's homemade brownies.

Breakfast in the Manor, says Rob, is a healthy vegetarian feast. It's served to guests at 9:00 a.m. and includes choices such as baked French toast, an egg frittata, homemade granola, Greek yogurt, pastries, bagels and muffins, plus fresh fruit and hot beverages. The herbs often come from the gardens outside your window. The coffee is organic fair trade. For earlier risers or those on the go who want to skip the big breakfast, a lighter meal is available between 7:00 and 10:00 a.m. that includes cereals and that fabulous homemade granola, juices and hot beverages. There are always options to satisfy people avoiding gluten as well.

If you stay in the Guest House, a picnic-basket breakfast will be delivered to your door between 7:00 and 7:30 a.m., which will include homemade granola, pastries, juice and your choice of a hot beverage.

Adapting our gardens for our aging selves and our changing earth
By Elaine Herbert

Everything changes. In forty years of coaxing soil, earth, seed, sun and water into art, I have learned that transience is the truth.

I've cultivated many different gardens. At the height of my rose obsession in the '90s I was tending four hundred shrubs, two hundred at the Manor and two hundred on a property close by. We would cut upward of fifty thousand roses for vases in rooms every June. Crazy and fabulous!

About ten years ago, I changed the inn's gardens to have more show for four full seasons, more flowering shrubs and an English cottage garden perennial border. I stopped using chemical food and pesticides and began to fill in with disease resistant, indigenous flora. I cultivated rich, worm-filled soil with naturally composted organic fertilizers. The gardens have been magnificent!

Now another change is on the way. Our next renovated garden must use less water, be sustainable, affordable, responsible, but still beautiful (I am still a gardener!). Global climate change trumps my classic lavish gardening style. Then there's this: I am now no longer forty years old. I'm in my sixties! So less maintenance is also a reality. Clearly, something's gotta give.

So my gardening journey returns to the beginning: simplicity.

The upcoming garden transitions will include more sweeping beds of beautiful foliage (enough deadheading already!), ornamental perennial grasses, sedums, hardy prairie flowers. We plan three stages, three springtime renovations, to scale back the gardens by about half. Everywhere. Just gotta be.

Maybe we'll add stepping stones with herbs that give up scent as you walk through.

Everything changes.

This is a great option for guests who are not big breakfast eaters, need to leave their rooms early or don't want to leave their rooms at all until it's time to check out.

Besides their passion for innkeeping, Elaine and Rob love gardening. The Manor and Guest House are surrounded by their spectacular gardens, and you'll often find one of them with garden tools in hand, pruning, picking and adding new finds. Do save some time to smell the flowers. A couple of hours spent sitting amid the peaceful beauty of their flourishing plantings will do wonders for your blood pressure.

Vitals

rooms: 11 in the Manor, 6 in the Guest House, all with private baths

pets permitted: no

pets in residence: none

open season: April 1 to November 1

rates: $145 to $325. Lower rates are available in spring and fall and Monday through Wednesday nights.

e-mail: elaine@yeltonmanor.com

web site: www.yeltonmanor.com

owners/innkeepers:
Elaine Herbert and Robert Kripaitis
140 North Shore Drive
South Haven, MI 49090
269-637-5220

Whitehall

We'll never know if it was Mrs. O'Leary's cow who started the great fire in Chicago in 1871, but we do know that it burned for two days and destroyed more than 3 square miles. Luckily, builders were able to look to Michigan for a seemingly endless supply of pine to rebuild the devastated city. Mills around White Lake, cradled by the cities of Whitehall to the east and Montague to the west, were already receiving logs from operations up river. When the demand suddenly increased, so did output from the mills.

But the pine supply was not endless. By the end of the nineteenth century, the forests that had covered much of the northern half of the state were all but gone. Mills closed, and the bustling twin cities quieted down considerably. A century later they are in full swing again, and this time the draw is activities in the cities themselves and the abundant natural resources that surround them.

Today Whitehall and Montague are known for quaint shops and excellent marinas, artistic and cultural events and four seasons of outdoor activities, including ice fishing in deep winter. The city of Whitehall owns the historic Howmet Playhouse, which offers live theater and concerts throughout the year. The Arts Council of White Lake holds free concerts at the Montague band shell in the summer and classes and art exhibitions at its Nuveen Community Center for the Arts year-round.

Blue Lake Fine Arts Camp, 15 minutes away, hosts talented students from around the world who attend classes and give concerts during the summer. Michigan's Adventure, the state's largest amusement and water park, is just east of town. Abandoned railroads have been converted to miles of scenic, paved bike trails, which are linked to a network of trails throughout the state. The historic White River Light Station, perched on the south side of the channel where White Lake flows into Lake Michigan, is a museum. And some of the state's most beautiful sugar sand beaches stretch for miles along the Lake Michigan shore. Glorious cross-country ski trails are as close as Muskegon State Park, about 15 minutes to the south, and they are lighted at night.

Clustered in Whitehall, a stone's throw from each other, are three fine bed-and-breakfast homes, which offer history, hospitality and unique specialties.

WHITEHALL

A Finch Nest Bed and Breakfast

Helen Fink had a good feeling about this 1868 house as soon as she saw it. In fact, she says, she fell in love with it.

Helen had retired from teaching special education. Her husband, Andy, had retired from practicing law, and they had been thinking of opening a bed-and-breakfast home. "If you like to cook and entertain, you've already honed a lot of the skills that an innkeeper needs!," Helen told me with her characteristic enthusiasm during a recent visit to A Finch Nest. She and Andy looked at several buildings across the country, especially historic structures. Although they lived in Connecticut, they were open to moving just about anywhere. Michigan was especially attractive to them because Andy was raised in the state and has family on the east side.

This home had been owned by several families over its many decades and had, for a time, served as a boardinghouse for a local tannery, which housed visiting dignitaries there. It had been "modernized" with dropped ceilings, and the once gleaming maple floors had been painted black or carpeted over—or both. But Helen saw beyond all that. She especially liked the fact that the carriage house, where she envisioned their living quarters, is connected to the main house. She told Andy about it, and he went to see it.

"He called me from the pub," remembers Helen. "He said, 'We are having a $2 pitcher of beer!,' and I said, 'Buy the property!'" It was a great choice for us—a happy event.

They launched a substantial renovation and created three lovely guest rooms—one on the first floor and two on the second. Each is bright and airy, and their soft, neutral colors make them feel very tranquil. They are furnished with a comfortable mix of traditional styles plus stunning antique pieces, and the hardwood floors have been restored to their original beauty. Each guest room is named for little wild birds. I

especially like the collection of framed Audubon prints over the brass bed in the first-floor Indigo Bunting Room. The antique East Lake bed in the Purple Finch Room is gorgeous.

Each room has a large, attached private bath with both a whirlpool tub and a shower with a "rain" shower head, plus thick towels and plush terry robes—a combination that makes the baths very luxurious. The Goldfinch Room's tub is big enough for two. Spacious, contemporary bathrooms in a nineteenth-century home . . . what a great idea!

Guests love to gather in the large corner parlor on the first floor, and to sit by the wood-burning fireplace there when it's chilly. When the weather is mild, they enjoy the garden at the back of the house, which is anchored by an outdoor porch. It's Helen's first garden, and she describes it as more of a meadow with a small pond. It's lovely and peaceful, and there are several places where you can sit and enjoy the view.

Andy has taken up bread making, and you'll taste his specialties at breakfast. "Aren't I lucky?," says Helen, smiling. "Andy is smart and funny *and* he bakes bread!" Breakfast includes their special blend Finch Nest coffee, freshly squeezed juice and fresh fruits in season plus hot dishes such as Helen's signature rustic tarts. They are similar to quiches with a variety of vegetables and herbs from the garden. The eggs come from a local farmer.

The Finks offer several packages with lodging that can include options for shopping, golf, dinner and playhouse tickets. Hikers and bicyclists like the trail package, which includes being dropped off any-place they desire along the 25-mile bike trail that runs north of town with a packed picnic lunch. The house is also well suited for small groups that rent all three guest rooms. "We had six delightful women here who took the whole house for three days," Helen recalled of a craft-ing group that had stayed with her the week before my visit. "They crafted day and night. It was great fun!"

A Finch Nest sits in the middle of a quiet residential neighborhood. It's about four blocks to downtown Whitehall, and that's another reason guests like staying here. They can walk to the shops, restaurants and a vintage ice cream parlor, and to the historic Howmet Playhouse.

A few years ago Helen spearheaded a project to renovate a vintage caboose that located next to the White Lake Area Chamber of Com-merce, which is housed in the former train depot. When the Caboose Museum was completed, people started talking about the next proj-ect—a small twentieth-century building that was the office and apoth-ecary shop of Dr. John Meinhardi. In the early 1900s, it was located on Mears, the main north-south street in Whitehall. At some point, it was moved to the back of the lot, and that's where it stayed until July 2011, when it was moved again—this time amid much celebration—to a site next to the Caboose Museum. Andy created the We Can Do This Com-pany, a nonprofit organization that is helping to raise funds to restore it. Volunteers and local trades companies have been working on the structure, and when finished it will be a little walk-through museum.

Besides being an innkeeper and restorer of historic buildings, Helen is a marriage cleric of the Unitarian Church, and she loves to officiate at weddings, renewals of vows and commitment ceremonies.

Vitals

rooms: 3 with private baths

pets permitted: no

pets in residence: none

open season: year-round

rates: $120 to $140

e-mail: afinchnest@chartermi.net

website: www.afinchnest.com

owners/innkeepers:
Helen and Andy Fink
415 South Division
Whitehall, MI 49461
231-893-5323

WHITEHALL

Cocoa Cottage Bed and Breakfast

What's in a name?

Well, in this case, it's a good indication of some of the great food you're going to have here, so let's talk chocolate!

Lisa Tallarico created a unique hot fudge recipe as a holiday tradition for family, friends and coworkers. Then a friend asked if he could buy several jars of it for his sales team—three hundred, to be exact. Lisa obliged, and that was the genesis for commercial production of Mama Tallarico's Hot Fudge and, ultimately, for the Cocoa Cottage Bed and Breakfast.

Lisa is an artist and designer who grew up in Lansing. She was working at Hallmark Cards in Kansas City when she met Larry Robertson. He had owned an 80-acre dude ranch in Colorado for several years and later apprenticed at a five-star bed-and-breakfast inn in Kansas City. "The innkeepers took me under their wing and taught me the business," he remembers, "especially customer service and style." He loved the work.

When Lisa and Larry got together, they combined their dreams and talents. Lisa wanted an old house to restore, preferably near Lake Michigan, where she had spent a lot of time, and Larry was interested in opening a B&B. They spent months looking for just the right place, and the search led them to an arts and crafts bungalow in Whitehall that was built in 1912.

"We didn't know much about the style, but the house spoke to us," remembers Larry. "We loved the location and its proximity to Whitehall's downtown. We thought it had potential." The two began learning everything they could about the arts and crafts period—house designs, fabrics, furniture, colors and even the philosophy. They traveled the country looking at other A&C houses and attending symposiums on their restoration. Armed with volumes of knowledge and the desire to

re-create an authentic arts and crafts residence, they spent nearly ten years completing the careful restoration of their home, and they opened for B&B guests in 2002.

What you'll likely notice as soon as you step inside is the warmth of the wood and the historically accurate colors that Lisa and Larry selected. Many of the walls are covered with arts and crafts reproduction wallpapers by Bradbury & Bradbury. The original oak columns and plate rails have been scrubbed and waxed to reveal their rich grain. When the weather turns cool, the original brick fireplace in the living room is stoked first thing in the morning, and it's the last thing tended to at night, providing a warm and inviting area in which to read and relax. In keeping with the style, the living and dining rooms are furnished with original and reproduction arts and crafts period furniture, lighting, pottery and floor coverings. The original west-facing three-season porch has a comfortable cottage-style decor and is a delightful place to enjoy a morning cup of coffee or the sunset.

There are four guest rooms named for famous chocolatiers. The first-floor Ghirardelli suite, just off the living room, has classic arts and crafts decor and a private bath with an oversize whirlpool tub. On the second floor, you'll find the Hershey Room with an all-American up-

A style is born

The ats and crafts movement started in Great Britain around 1860 and continued to influence styles until the 1930s. It developed as a backlash to both the Industrial Revolution and the fussiness of Victorian design. More than just a style, it became a philosophy that advocated for social reforms and a simple life. As architects and homeowners eschewed machined work and gaudy finishes, artists and craftsmen found a market for their trade that valued simple, clean lines. Wood was used generously, and it was often waxed instead of stained or painted. Colors were inspired by nature. Dyes were made from natural materials such as cranberries and bark. Trees and grass lent their palettes of warm, rich greens, taupes and browns. In the United States, the movement fostered the craftsman, mission, bungalow and prairie styles and influenced everything from pottery and jewelry to sculpture, furniture and fabrics.

---

north-cabin look complete with a king-size log bed. The Cadbury Room has a white wrought-iron bed and touches of an English garden. And the Godiva Room is a sweet taste of luxury with its brass bed and private balcony. Each room has a private bath, luxurious toiletries, plush cotton bathrobes and beach towels. I love the tradition of turn-down service here, along with evening port and, of course, handmade chocolates.

As for the food at Cocoa Cottage, "We always include chocolate . . . even at breakfast!" says Larry, who is house chef. He and Lisa have become experts on chocolate—where it comes from, how it is processed and when it tastes best. "I know as much about chocolate as I do arts and crafts!," Larry says happily as he gives me a bit of a primer. Cocoa beans, it turns out, only grow in a region about 10 degrees north or south of the equator. To make their signature Cocoa Cottage chocolates, Lisa and Larry use a cocoa powder that is custom blended for them. It uses cocoa beans from a single region because, Larry explains, the area where cocoa beans grow is as important to the flavor of chocolate as the location of grapes is to the flavor of wine.

If you arrive at Cocoa Cottage by 5:00 p.m., you'll get your first taste of the chocolate specialties served here. From 5:00 to 6:00 p.m., Larry offers wine, hors d'oeuvres and a chocolate dessert such as chocolate decadence, chocolate truffle tart or chocolate mousse in chocolate cups.

Chocolate zucchini bread, Mama Tallarico's Hot Fudge and fresh strawberries are a staple at the breakfast table. You might also be treated to chocolate chip waffles, stuffed chocolate French toast, or the inn's signature cottage eggs, which are so pretty guests run to get their cameras! Larry creates a potato-crusted asparagus quiche for his gluten-free guests or lemon ricotta pancakes served with fresh heritage black raspberries from Lisa's garden. In warm months, guests enjoy breakfast on the pergola-enclosed patio surrounded by horticultural delights that begin with a profusion of sweetly scented wisteria blooms in June.

Do check out the Cocoa Cottage packages. From murder mysteries and girls' night out (no boys allowed except Larry) to Chocolate 101, they are designed to entertain, inform and inspire. For an intimate, romantic, culinary experience, consider reserving a package called Table 223. It includes a candlelit, multicourse dinner that Larry builds according to your preferences, and it is served with wines that complement each course. All you have to do is relax and enjoy your time together.

The B&B is also lovely place for small weddings, and Lisa and Larry create desserts for all occasions. By the way, if you get a chance to try one of their chocolate peanut butter truffles, do. They are melt-in-your-mouth wonderful!

Vitals

rooms: 4 rooms with private baths

pets permitted: no

pets in residence: none

open season: yearround

rates: $129 to $189

e-mail: innkeeper@cocoacottage.com

website: www.cocoacottage.com

owners/innkeepers:
Lisa Tallarico and Larry Robertson
223 South Mears Avenue
Whitehall, MI 49461
231-893-0674
800-204-7596

WHITEHALL

White Swan Inn

On my first visit to the White Swan Inn many years ago, I walked from room to room admiring the three sets of huge pocket doors, the original wooden carpenter's lace and the handsome walnut staircase leading to the second floor.

"We were very lucky," owner Cathy Russell explained. "When we bought the inn, many of the home's original features were still in place. The woodwork wasn't painted, and most of the original interior shutters were still on the windows.

And that just begins the list of turn-of-the-century treasures here. The floor in the dining room, for example, is pegged oak parquet with a border of inlaid cherry, maple, oak and walnut. There's a wide, built-in corner cabinet reminiscent of those found in eighteenth-century colonial homes. And there are pocket *windows* that slide up into the wall above when they are opened.

If you visited before 1995, you would have known it as The Time Keepers Inn, named for the clock shop that the former owners operated in the front parlor. You'll find the reception area for the inn there now, along with a small gift shop, which offers whimsical and decorator items and White Lake memorabilia so you can take home tangible reminders of your visit. Beyond the parlor is the living room, bathed in the light that pours in through a deep south-facing bay window.

The home is filled with a mix of antiques and contemporary pieces that complement the classic lines of this 1884 beauty. Four guest rooms are located on the second floor, and three are very large. The Cygnet Suite includes an attached bathing room with a hydromassage whirlpool tub and a separate shower. I am especially fond of the summery Jasmine Room, furnished in white wicker. The Covell Room has a rare, original, claw-foot tub with an oak rim. The petite Mariner Room is one step down and tucked at the back of the house—cozy, quiet and very

private. A sitting room at the top of the stairs is furnished in a nautical theme to accommodate the Russells' collection of sailing paraphernalia, including amazing model ships that Cathy's husband Ron creates by hand.

Breakfast time is flexible to accommodate guests' activities that day. It's full and hot and fabulous. Cathy is a great baker!

At any time of the day, porch sitting and people watching are engaging pastimes here. A wide veranda wraps the front and side of the inn, and it is as welcoming in the morning when you're enjoying a cup of coffee as it is in the afternoon when you're sampling Cathy's homemade shortbread or fresh-from-the-oven cookies. The historic Howmet Theater is directly across the street.

When the Russells bought the inn, they changed its name to the White Swan Inn in honor of the flocks of the graceful birds that gather on White Lake, just a few blocks away. With its success, they added Swan Cottage, an adorable two-bedroom guesthouse available for extended stays and perfect for travelers with young children and pets. It's located just 2 minutes away in Montague and has everything you need for settling in, including a full kitchen, dining room, washer and dryer and fenced backyard.

Then . . . wishing to expand a little more, they purchased a 40-foot trawler-style yacht, christened her *Third Swan* and opened her for dock-

side accommodations and cruises. *Third Swan* has two staterooms, each with a private head, and a full galley. The screened aft deck is a great spot for happy hour, and the flying bridge offers a 360-degree view of White Lake.

Ron is a lifelong sailor, and he holds a Coast Guard–issued Masters License. He offers several charter options by reservation, from romantic sunset cruises to history tours around White Lake, which can be arranged with or without accommodations. If you're feeling adventurous, consider reserving a cruise north

along the shore of Lake Michigan to Pentwater or south to Grand Haven.

Vitals

> *rooms:* 4 in the inn with private baths. Swan Cottage has 2 bed-rooms and 1 bath, and the *Third Swan* has 2 staterooms with private baths.

pets permitted: no

pets in residence: 2 cats

open season: year-round

rates: $125 to $185 for the inn. Ask about cottage and yacht rates

e-mail: stay@whiteswaninn.com

website: www.whiteswaninn.com

owners/innkeepers:
  Cathy and Ron Russell
  303 South Mears
  Whitehall, MI 49461
  231-894-5169
  888-948-7926

HEARTLAND:
THE CENTRAL
LOWER PENINSULA

Alma
Saravilla Bed and Breakfast

Battle Creek
Greencrest Manor

Coldwater
Chicago Pike Inn and Spa

Eaton Rapids
The English Inn

Grandville
*Prairieside Suites Luxury Bed
and Breakfast*

Jonesville
Munro House Bed and Breakfast

Jugville (White Cloud)
The Shack

Kalamazoo
Kalamazoo House Bed and Breakfast

Marshall
The National House Inn

Mount Pleasant
*Country Chalet and Edelweiss Haus
Ginkgo Tree Inn*

Union City
The Victorian Villa Inn

ALMA

Saravilla Bed and Breakfast

Some people get a place setting of silverware or a roasting pan for a wedding present. In 1894 Sara Wright got a three-story, late-Victorian-style home as a wedding present from her lumber baron father, Ammi Willard Wright. It was a summer home, actually, and when the construction was completed, Wright had it trimmed out with splendid imported woods, leaded-glass windows, light fixtures and hand-painted wall coverings, including a canvas border painted in Paris. It was lovely, but Sara wanted more space. She needed room to entertain, so a Dutch colonial wing was added with a 1,200-square-foot first-floor ballroom.

The home was, apparently, Ammi's way of encouraging Sara to come to Alma to visit him, but Sara was not entranced with the town. After her father died, she closed the house and never returned. It went through many changes of ownership and uses through the decades. For about forty years, it served as a nursing facility. One owner added an eighteen-room wing for business purposes, and when the business failed, an Amish group accepted the opportunity to remove the wing in exchange for keeping the building materials.

Linda and Jon Darrow learned several years ago that Sara Wright's fabulous house was for sale, and they went to look at it, largely out of curiosity. Even after so much time had passed, the stately mansion retained many of its original architectural features plus interior finish work such as built-in glass-front cabinets, quarter-sawn oak paneling and beamed ceilings. The Darrows realized they were looking at an 11,000-square-foot treasure, and they wondered who would ever buy such a huge home. When the realtor mentioned that it might be usable as a bed and breakfast, the spark was lit. They bought it in 1990 and embarked on the challenging process of restoring what could be saved and redoing what could not, replacing plumbing and wiring and opening rooms as they completed them.

The highlands of . . . Alma?

Yes! The residents of Alma host an annual Highland Festival, which brings together members of Scottish clans and thousands of enthusiastic onlookers for two days packed with food and dancing, Celtic music, caber tossing (you'll have to ask), bagpipe playing and all things Scottish.

For something close to canine poetry, watch the herding events where border collies, working in a finely tuned partnership with their trainers, round up sheep.

This very popular festival began in the late 1960s and takes place over Memorial Day weekend.

There are eight guest rooms on the second and third floors now. Many are quite spacious—large enough, in fact, for a queen-size or double bed plus a twin bed and a sitting area. Some rooms can hold an additional rollaway as well. That much sleeping space in one room often makes it possible for guests traveling with children or friends to stay in the same room together. Linda says when all the rooms are full, the inn will accommodate twenty-five adults and kids.

The furnishings represent several vintage periods, and many of the beds are covered with pretty quilts. Each room has a private bath. Some are attached, and some are across the hall. Robes have been thoughtfully provided for guests.

For a romantic treat, reserve the Ammi Wright Suite with its iron king-size canopy bed, a little sitting room with a wood-burning fireplace and a private bath with a whirlpool tub. The Turret Room also has an original wood-burning fireplace and a large bathroom with a whirlpool tub. I stayed in the Orchard Room, which is furnished with both a queen-size bed and a twin, a handsome bird's-eye maple dresser and pretty floral prints. The big detached bathroom is right around the corner.

As you might expect in a home this large, there are several common areas. The library is stocked with collections of books from Linda's and Jon's families, and when it's chilly, the fireplace in this cozy room is usually ablaze. You're welcome to play pool in the billiard room or soak away the day's cares in the hot tub in the sun-room. A first-floor guest kitchen has a microwave oven and refrigerator, and you'll find cookies waiting there for you each evening.

Then there's that amazing ballroom. Scrapbookers love it. There is so much space, and they can spread out their materials on worktables that the inn provides. The ballroom is also a favorite location for weddings and receptions and all kinds of meetings and special events. It has another of the home's original fireplaces and a pretty Victorian parlor set in a sitting area at one end.

In keeping with the grand style of Saravilla, breakfast is served on antique china in the formal dining room. It always includes a hot entrée, baked goods and fruit. I loved the fresh fruit with yogurt and could have happily lingered over coffee all morning in that beautiful room. Breakfast times are very flexible. "We accommodate everyone from business travelers to couples looking for a weekend getaway," explained Linda, "Some guests need to be up and out very early, and others want to sleep in. We let them decide when they want to eat."

Alma is located in the center of the Lower Peninsula. Besides being a convenient stopover on the way to other places, the city is home to Alma College, which offers musical and theatrical performances, as do both the Gratiot County Playhouse and Central Michigan University, just 20 minutes away. The area hosts several festivals throughout the year, including Alma's famous Highland Festival and the Masonic Festival.

Vitals

rooms: 8 with private baths

pets permitted: no

pets in residence: none

open season: year-round

rates: $99 to $169

e-mail: ljdarrow@saravilla.com

website: www.saravilla.com

owners/innkeepers:
Linda and Jon Darrow
633 N. State Street
Alma, MI 48801
989-463-4078

BATTLE CREEK

Greencrest Manor

Close your eyes. Now open them. Yes, that's a perfect French Normandy chateau, and it really is just a few miles outside of Battle Creek. You can close your eyes again. It won't disappear. Greencrest Manor is here to stay and only because intrepid owners Kathy and Tom Van Daff saved this treasure from the wrecking ball.

The home was built in 1935 and was intended as the private residence of Nellie and George Burt. The couple had picked a quiet area on a hill overlooking St. Mary's Lake, which was a favorite picnic spot of theirs. Then the unthinkable happened—George died before construction began. Nellie vowed to continue the project as a tribute to him, patterning the home after an estate in northwestern France, with all the details expected of a proper Normandy estate, including iron gates, stone walls, formal gardens and a matching carriage house.

In the 1960s the home was purchased by the Catholic Church and used as a seminary for twenty years. Then it was sold again. Left empty, and it began to suffer serious damage. When Tom and Kathy first crossed the crumbling threshold, it was only because the door was ajar, and they ignored the signs declaring it condemned.

Today the oval two-story foyer with a spiral staircase leading to the cantilevered second-floor landing makes a spectacular first impression. You'd never guess for a moment what Greencrest looked like when the Van Daffs bought it in 1987.

"Floors and ceilings were missing, and fireplace mantles had been pulled out and sold," remembers Kathy. Doors were gone, windows were boarded over and the long-neglected grounds were a mess. What followed was part magic, part vision, and a ton of hard work.

With their combined skills in woodworking, gardening and decorating, and with the home's original blueprints in hand, Kathy and Tom spent thousands of hours repairing original features such as pecan pan-

The Old World practice of espaliering trees

As you walk around the grounds and gardens at Greencrest, you'll see apple and pear trees that have been pruned and trained to grow horizontally on a flat plane. This ancient horticultural practice, called espalier, grew out of a need to conserve space. It could also extend the growing season when the tree was planted against a wall that would retain the day's heat. The result is both artistic and fruitful.

The espaliered fruit trees at Greencrest, along with carefully tended vegetable gardens, grapevines and tiny banty hens, provide fresh ingredients for your breakfast.

eling in the library, French doors, and the estate's evocative stone walls, fountains and terraced garden. They searched for, and found, chandeliers, fireplace mantels and wall coverings that complement the Normandy style, and gradually the home came back to life.

As rooms were completed, Kathy and Tom furnished them with English and French antiques and reproductions. They added fine carpets, books and art, plus collections of silver and pottery. They even obtained a pair of amethyst Fu dogs from the Nellie Burt estate. Because the transformation of the estate is so complete, it is easy to assume that it has always been maintained in its 1930s state of grandeur. Each room, with its luxurious fabrics, artwork and furnishings, gives the feeling that Nellie herself may have just stepped out for the evening and lent you her gracious home. Kathy and Tom have paid great attention to the details here, and the effect is breathtaking.

Eight luxurious sleeping rooms are located on the second and third floors. Three are very large and have spacious sitting areas. The Burt Suite, Nellie's original room, is dressed with Ralph Lauren fabrics and has windows on three sides plus a large dressing room. If you're traveling with another couple, consider reserving the Geranium and Lilac Rooms, which are located in a private wing of the house. Each has a sink in the room, and they share a bath.

Three under-the-eaves rooms on the third floor have views out of the home's original oval windows. I particularly love the red and cream toile headboard and linens in Fern's Room. All of the sleeping rooms, with their elegant designer fabrics, art and accessories, remind me of accommodations in fine European hotels. Do take a look at the photos on the website!

Breakfast is served in the formal dining room in the warm light of a fabulous antique brass and crystal chandelier. It includes entrées such as a quiche or cheese soufflé, fresh fruit, a variety of pastries and breads, plus homemade jams. Being so close to the cereal capital of the world, you'll also have a choice of cereals.

While Greencrest Manor is a splendid place for a romantic getaway, business travelers love the inn and all its amenities as well. Each room has cable TV, a writing desk, Wi-Fi and a sitting area, and the common areas give you plenty of opportunity to work someplace other than in your room.

The inn is especially well suited for small corporate gatherings, and I can only imagine how pleasant and productive a company retreat would be here! The location is ideal—less than 10 minutes from Battle Creek and about an hour from the Grand Rapids airport. The Van Daffs will provide the tables and chairs you need for up to twenty-five people in theater seating or twenty at round tables. It's quiet and peaceful here, thanks in part to the original 18-inch-thick walls and floors, and the grounds are truly inspiring. Meals can be arranged, and water and sodas with meals are complimentary.

As you might guess, Greencrest is very popular with brides, and it can host outdoor weddings from spring through fall for up to two hundred guests. Small weddings that can be held inside are welcome any time of the year. Kathy can provide contacts for all the special services you'll need to create an event that is stress free and storybook memorable.

Vitals

rooms: 8 sleeping rooms, 6 with private baths, 2 share 1 bath

pets permitted: no

pets in residence: none

open season: year-round

rates: $135 to $275

e-mail: klbvd@comcast.net

website: www.greencrestmanor.com

owners/innkeepers:
Kathy and Tom Van Daff
6174 Halbert Road
Battle Creek, MI 49017
269-962-8633

COLDWATER

Chicago Pike Inn and Spa

If you've driven through Coldwater in the last twenty years, it's likely you remember this stately colonial home, which sits handsomely on an acre of land at the edge of the city. Its massive Greek revival columns, first- and second-floor verandas and daffodil yellow exterior are traffic stoppers. And owner Nancy Krajny says she walks through this home each day with the appreciation of someone seeing it for the first time, amazed that it's really hers!

Route 12, which runs east and west through the center of Coldwater, was originally a trail between Chicago and Detroit and later was used by pioneers heading west. Michigan became a state in 1837, but because of Coldwater's convenient location on the way to other places, this area was populated with trading posts as early as 1825. Morris G. Clarke was a successful Coldwater merchant when he asked Chicago architect Ashbury Buckley, known for the summer homes he designed on Mackinac Island in the late 1800s, to design this mansion. It was completed in 1903 for the astronomical sum of $15,000.

Mr. Clarke lived there with his wife Margaret and their three children until his passing in 1927. When Margaret died in 1936, her two sons sold the property, and it was run as a rooming house until 1988. Harold and Jane Schultz bought the home and spent a year restoring it to its original splendor, then filled it with the kinds of elegantly styled furnishings that likely graced the estate when the Clarkes lived there. Many of the antiques they chose were purchased in Europe. Battenberg lace was shipped in by the bolt for custom-made curtains, and they opened for bed-and-breakfast guests in 1989.

Nancy purchased the inn in 2005—complete. "The Schultzes told me to just bring my toothbrush and I'd be in business!," she says with a smile. She was even handed the recipes that guests had come to love over the years. Nancy was used to making people feel good—she had

Giving back

Each year Nancy holds a rejuvenating retreat at the inn for women who are in treatment for cancer or were in treatment the previous year. She secures sponsors to help underwrite the weekend, so there is no cost to her guests. She donates all the food and schedules music, speakers and makeup and skin care consultants who demonstrate ways to counteract the side effects of treatment. She also maintains a wig bank for women who have lost their hair, and she styles each wig so it suits its new owner perfectly.

The guests arrive Friday afternoon, and for two days the inn is given over completely to honoring and pampering them. The weekend ends on Sunday afternoon with an uplifting nondenominational spiritual service.

been a hairdresser since 1974—and she decided very quickly to add the option of spa services for her guests. The mansion's stylish carriage house is just a few steps from the back door, and it already had two beautiful guest rooms with whirlpool tubs on its second floor, so Nancy converted the first floor into her beauty salon and massage room. The pampering extras have been a hit!

From the moment I stepped onto that amazing veranda, I confess, I was smitten with this inn. Everywhere you look there are marvelous original architectural details and miles of rich cherry wood trim. And do pause for a few minutes at the bottom of the grand staircase to take in the intricate leaded-glass window that all but fills the wall at the landing. The rooms are large and airy and softened with oriental rugs, period wall coverings and elegant fabrics. Brides love Miss Sophia's Suite at the top of the stairs. Its sitting room includes an original yellow-tiled fireplace and oak mantle, and it offers plenty of room for the bride and her attendants to dress for the ceremony. The small, two-room Hired Girls Suite is pure country comfort with its white iron bed, red plaid wall coverings and poplar floors. The Stableman's Room in the Carriage House has a primitive look with rough plastered walls and pegs that hold straw hats, suspenders and horse harnesses. The pencil-post bed is covered with an antique quilt.

Nancy believes her guests come to the inn in search of an experience and an opportunity to step back to a gentler time. You can expect to be well cared for here from the moment you arrive until you check out. Breakfast, for example, is a two-course sit-down pleasure that takes

at least an hour, and Nancy offers two seating times to accommodate those who like to get started early and those who want to sleep late. You can look forward to treats such as peach sorbet served with homemade zucchini bread and lemon chiffon French toast with homemade lemon curd. Nancy sits on the advisory board for the culinary arts program at the Branch Area Career Center and is a big supporter of eating locally made, locally grown food. She has also adapted a lot of her recipes to be sugar and gluten free.

For business travelers and those leaving early, Nancy sets out juice, fruit, pastries and coffee. And if you're in a hurry but not yet hungry, she offers a truly thoughtful touch—breakfast-to-go boxes.

Guests of the inn can also make reservations for a four-course private dinner, served in the dining room in the glow of candlelight. Ask Nancy about menu options. As with breakfast, she can adapt the romantic meal to all kinds of dietary needs, and you're welcome to furnish your own wine or champagne.

The combination of the size of the inn, its commercial kitchen and Nancy's resourcefulness makes it a great location for receptions, showers and parties. Nancy can host up to sixty people indoors, and outdoors, she says, the sky's the limit! Wedding couples love being able to schedule their whole event here. From manicures, pedicures, massages and hairstyling in preparation to the wedding ceremony, reception and lodging for family and friends, everything is available on site, and Nancy will coordinate the details so the celebration is seamless.

Antiquing, as you may already know, is big in this area. Nearby Allen and Shipshewana, Indiana, are renowned for their antique shops and malls. Nancy can direct you to local festivals, county fairs and the spectacular 1882 Tibbits Opera House in Coldwater, the second-oldest theater in Michigan. It has been undergoing a masterful restoration and is home to a variety of theater and cultural events.

Vitals

rooms: 8 with private baths, 6 in the main house and 2 in the Carriage House.

pets permitted: no

pets in residence: yes, limited to the innkeeper's quarters

open season: year-round

rates: $119 to $195

e-mail: nancy@chicagopikeinn.com

website: www.chicagopikeinn.com

owner and innkeeper:
Nancy Krajny
215 East Chicago Street
Coldwater, MI 49036
517-279-8744
800-471-0501

EATON RAPIDS

The English Inn

Northern Michigan had its copper and lumber barons. Southern Michigan had auto barons, and Irving Reuter was one of them. He was general manager of the Oldsmobile Corporation in 1927, when he began constructing his Tudor revival mansion on 15 rolling acres alongside the Grand River. He was also an inventor and one of the original ten investors in General Motors. Irving and his wife Janet called the home Medovue, and from 1928 to 1936, they lived large and entertained lavishly. The bucolic setting, formal gardens and Old World architecture must have made this estate feel a continent away, yet it's only a short, half-hour drive from Lansing.

The Reuters were here less than ten years when Irving retired and the couple moved out of state. From 1940 to 1962, the Catholic Church owned it. The Reverend Joseph H. Albers, the first bishop of the Diocese of Lansing, used it as his private residence. In 1989 new owners renovated extensively and turned the home into an inn with a fine restaurant on the first floor.

Gary Nelson had been in the hospitality business for twenty-five years when the inn came up for sale. He and his wife Donna always enjoyed historic structures. In fact Gary oversaw work on the Studebaker mansion in South Bend, Indiana, when it was converted from a home to a restaurant, and they had been looking for a place in Michigan where they could undertake a similar project. "I saw an article about The English Inn in the newspaper and showed it to Gary," remembers Donna. "It was already a working inn and restaurant, and it seemed like the perfect next step for us." Gary agreed, and they bought it. That was in 1996, and within a few years its elegant guest rooms and extraordinary food were attracting double the number of guests it was hosting when they took it over. The second generation has now come onboard. Son Erik Nelson, who graduated from Michigan State University's School

of Hospitality Business, recently joined the endeavor as innkeeper and managing partner.

Lunch and dinner are served in the first-floor living room, the original dining room and the sun-room, and all three give you a sense of the opulent life the Reuters created here. The original coffered ceiling in the living room has been beautifully preserved, as has the Honduran mahogany paneled walls and black marble fireplace. The original dining room overlooks the estate's formal gardens, and the Thames Room, that bright and beautiful sun-room, has leaded windows on three sides and views of both the gardens and the river.

Lunch offerings include a number of intriguing dishes such as wild mushroom pappardelle pasta with baby spinach, truffle oil and pine nuts; a variety of sandwiches; a duck cassoulet; and British specialties such as a Cornish pasty and fish and chips.

Dinner choices include tempting appetizers such as caviar for two and a delicate lobster bisque. Entrées include lobster stuffed walleye, stuffed quail, English Inn prime rib and chateaubriand for two. Lunch is available Monday through Friday. Dinner is served every evening, and a special five-course dinner is served all day Sunday.

One of my favorite spots in the inn is the pub on the lower level called the Oxford Library. Warm and intimate, it has a terrazzo floor, a low, beamed ceiling and a stone fireplace. Can you picture it? It's pure, cozy old English, complete with Dickensian pictures on the wall and a stone terrace just outside. If you're hungry, you can order from either the pub's or the dining room's menus.

Six guest rooms are located on the second floor, and they mirror the elegance of the first floor with fine linens and bedcovers, antiques and French and English accents. Most are quite large. They are named for people and places in England, and many have original architectural features such as Gothic doors and leaded-glass windows that overlook the gardens. The Windsor Room was the Reuters', master bedroom, and it has a gorgeous rose marble fireplace and a sitting area. One of the most unusual rooms I've seen is The Bath, named both for the village in England and for its features. When you enter it, you'll find yourself in one of the home's spacious original bathrooms complete with apple green ceramic tiles, a classic 1920s jetted shower, a lovely chandelier and a table for two! Walk through the bathroom and you'll come to the pretty sleeping room. It is thought that this is where the bishop slept, given the small religious painting on the ceiling over the bed.

Two cottages on the grounds of the inn have also been renovated for guests' use. Honeysuckle Cottage, originally the caretaker's home, has a large living room and three bedrooms, which can be rented together or separately. Each has a fireplace and a private bath with a jetted tub. Ivy Cottage is the estate's former milking house, and it is a perfect couple's getaway. It has a living room plus a sitting room with a fireplace that opens onto a bathroom with a vaulted ceiling and a jetted tub. In a nod to the preferences of today's travelers, beds in the inn and the cottages are queen- or king-size, and each room has cable TV.

Breakfast is served in the sun-room to guests of the inn and the cottages between 8:30 and 9:30 a.m. You'll also find coffee service at your door each morning.

A few years ago the Nelsons added a large banquet facility on the east lawn adjacent to the formal gardens. Its design was inspired by wineries the Nelsons fell in love with in France, and they christened it Medovue to honor the estate's original name. A large marble foyer sets the tone as soon as you enter. Palladium-style windows, chandeliers, artwork and tapestries in the ballroom provide the perfect backdrop for weddings and other special events.

Do take some time to stroll the grounds here. The original pergola still anchors one end of the gardens, and lawn croquet is set up next to the estate's original artesian well. The Grand River is just beyond. I am always touched by the efforts of innkeepers to preserve a bit of local history and the lifestyle that went with it. After almost ninety years, The English Inn seems every bit as gracious and charming as I imagine it was when the Reuters first opened its doors.

Vitals

rooms: 6 sleeping rooms in the inn and 3 in Honeysuckle Cottage with private baths, 1 guest cottage with a private bath.

pets permitted: no

pets in residence: none

open season: year-round, except Christmas Day and the Fourth of July

rates: $115 to $185

e-mail: info@englishinn.com

website: www.englishinn.com

owners:
Donna and Gary Nelson

innkeeper:
Erik Nelson
677 South Michigan Road
Eaton Rapids, MI 48827
517-663-2500
800-858-0598

GRANDVILLE

Prairieside Suites Luxury Bed and Breakfast

So you'd like to get away.

And you want someplace private, where you'll feel pampered and relaxed.

You might even hope to feel like you just landed in another part of the world—the French Riviera, for example, or Tuscany. Perhaps a hip loft in the Big Apple is more to your liking?

And let me guess. You want this treat because you're celebrating a birthday or anniversary, an engagement or an empty nest, or you just want a little romantic time together because gas was $1.29 a gallon the last time you went away without the children. You deserve it. And you only have a few days because your kids or your parents or your jobs really do need you, so if this magical place could be close to home, that would be even better.

Well, you're not alone. There's a growing trend among vacationers to seek a getaway that's not far away.

Cheri and Paul Antozak have created an amazing bed and breakfast located just a few minutes from shopping, movie theaters, restaurants and downtown Grand Rapids, and 20 minutes from Lake Michigan. "Many of our guests just can't get away for a week or two, but they can take a few days to come here to celebrate, relax, retreat and indulge themselves," says Cheri. "We offer a quiet haven to escape from the world, renew your energy and rekindle your relationship."

Cheri is a certified kitchen and bathroom designer and a licensed builder, and she's on the Michigan register of interior designers. Paul is a licensed builder and remodeling contractor. Since 1986 their "real" jobs have been remodeling homes through their company, Interiors by Cheri.

"I have had the opportunity to travel and stay in some of the best

hotels around the country," says Cheri, who went on a mission to create the perfect guest suite. "As a designer, I can't help but analyze how
any room can be made even better. I want our guests to feel instantly
comfortable because we've anticipated their needs. Paul and I are design
professionals who are in love and in business. That set the perfect stage
for creating a romantic bed and breakfast!"

They bought three houses on a corner in Grandville, including a
1920s Dutch colonial, which serves as the hub of the inn, and opened for
guests in 2002. There are five rooms in the main home and three in the
Prairie Annex house next door. And they are dreamy rooms. Each has a
king-size bed with designer linens, a whirlpool tub for two, a table for
two, an electric fireplace, an electric towel warmer and a private bath.
You'll also find a delightful beverage center with everything you need to
make coffee or cocoa, plus an ecofriendly wine chiller, a corkscrew and
bottle stopper, silverware, plates, a cheese slicer, glasses, a refrigerator
and so much more. Each room also has a flat-screen TV plus a DVD and
VCR player, and there is a huge library of movies and music for guests to
borrow. Oh yes, when the weather turns cold, there is a little plug you
can attach to the toilet seat so it's warmed. Some rooms also have jetted
showers, warmed tile floors and mirror defoggers in the bathroom.

The rooms have been buffered for sound with exceptionally thick
walls and floors and special sound-proofing materials. You won't hear
so much as the sound of a cabinet door slamming in your own room
because they have special soft closures. Two of the rooms are on the

lower level of the main home, which many guests prefer because of the complete sense of calming, away-from-it-all privacy they offer.

Each room has a theme taken from a special place somewhere around the world. Southern Mansion, just off the dining room, drew me in immediately. Its built-in whirlpool tub is anchored by four fluted columns and lit by a sparkling chandelier. French Riviera has handsome, built-in, dark wood cabinetry, which sets off the classic blue and white French country bedcovers and a canopy bed with brushed-nickel finish. I also love New York Loft with its contemporary lines, striking café au lait walls, a vessel sink and walk-in shower. The Loft is on the second floor and has several large windows, so Cheri gives you the option of enjoying that natural light or opting for privacy with room-darkening roman shades.

The grounds around and between the two buildings are landscaped with perennials, fragrant roses and lush hydrangeas. There is also a small terraced garden, which was overflowing with ripe tomatoes when I visited in September. And you can take in all this loveliness while you unwind on the double glider in the pergola or relax by the swimming pool.

Cheri offers three options for breakfast so you can choose what best suits you. A full, hot, plated breakfast is served at about 9:30 a.m. in the dining room of the main home, where you're likely to enjoy the company of other guests. For an extra charge, you can have it delivered to your room instead, and it will arrive around 10:00 a.m. You can also opt for a continental breakfast, which will be set up in your refrigerator

before you arrive so you can eat it anytime. When you reserve a room, you'll get a sheet that asks your breakfast preference, plus a checklist for foods—from gluten and dairy to mushrooms and meat—that you don't eat. It's thoughtful and thorough.

The central room of the main house is a combination sitting room and spotless, open kitchen with bar chairs at the counter. If you're an early riser and you plan to join other guests for breakfast in the dining room, feel free to arrive early, pour yourself a cup of coffee and have a chat with the cook!

If you want to make your stay even more memorable, check the website for all the special options you can add, from flowers and massage for two to chocolates, movie tickets and even hot pizza on arrival. Cheri and Paul have thought of everything, so you don't have to worry about anything.

While Prairieside Suites provides abundant amenities for a romantic retreat, it's also a favorite destination for business travelers who want to rest and recharge while on the road. The neighborhood is solidly suburban, and it's just a couple of blocks from Grandville's main street. The elementary school is across the street, the police station is one block over, and the library is a bit beyond that. A popular bike and walking trail nearby runs through town and connects to miles of trails across the state.

Vitals

rooms: 8 with private baths

pets permitted: in the Southern Mansion Room only

petsin residence: none

open season: year-round

rates: $199 to $289

e-mail: cheri@prairieside.com

website: www.prairieside.com

owners/innkeepers:
Cheri and Paul Antozak
3180 Washington Ave. SW
Grandville, MI 49418
616-538-9442

Munro House Bed and Breakfast

Step onto the grounds of the Munro House, close your eyes, and allow your thoughts to drift back to 1834. Twenty-year-old George C. Munro, son of a successful merchant and banker, had traveled that year from New York to the Territory of Michigan to make a living for himself. He had entered Yale University at sixteen but was forced to leave because of poor health, and he had become dissatisfied working as a clerk for his father. Michigan was a good choice for him. He was quickly engaged in mercantile and real estate business in Jackson, Lenawee, and Hillsdale counties, and Jonesville became his headquarters. Records show that the town had thirty or forty male inhabitants at the time, and perhaps Munro deemed that to be the sign of a town that would prosper.

Munro became a prominent and public man in southern Michigan. He traded with Baw Beese, the chief of the local Potawatomi. He ran flour mills and owned a hardware business. He worked as a contractor erecting roadbed and railroad buildings, and he farmed many acres. He also served as justice of the peace. When the Civil War broke out, he was engaged to recruit soldiers. He got involved in politics and education. He was a delegate to the Democratic Convention in Baltimore in 1860 and to the National Democratic Convention in St. Louis in 1876.

As I stand in the expansive double parlor of the house he built, I also learn this: he became deeply committed to helping men and women escape the bonds of slavery, and his home—this home—was a significant link in the Underground Railroad. While there is no recorded count, townspeople believe he and his family assisted hundreds.

Munro began building this home the same year he arrived in Michigan. It is the oldest house and first brick building in Hillsdale County. With its 12-foot ceilings on the first floor and ten fireplaces, it was an impressive and stately residence. It also held secrets known only to

those who needed to know: a false ceiling, a hidden room, large enough to hold twenty people, and a stone-walled tunnel leading from the base-ment to the carriage house. I put my hands on the remains of that tun-nel wall, cool to the touch in spite of it being 94°F outside. For a while I cannot speak. It is impossible not to be moved by this unassuming space that offered safety and hope to so many—a stop on the path to Windsor, Ontario, and freedom.

Owner Mike Venturini brings me back to the present with a smile. "And I get to live here!," he says. He will repeat this several times on my afternoon tour, because even though he has dwelt in the midst of this history since 1999, he is still in awe of it.

Mike and his wife Lori are from Appleton, Wisconsin, where both held corporate jobs. Mike traveled a lot and was ready for something new. His only criterion was that he wanted to be home at night. While booking reservations online for a trip to Italy, the couple got a pop-up ad for a bed and breakfast for sale in Jonesville. They decided to take a look. As Mike remembers it, he walked in the door of the Munro House and said, "I'm buying this. It feels like home." Ten weeks later they moved in.

There are seven sleeping rooms here, and each is beautifully decorated around a theme. Because Mike and Lori have different tastes in
furnishings, some rooms reflect the period of the home while others
are more contemporary. Clara's Room, for example, is quite modern
with its gas fireplace and two-person jetted tub. George's Room has a
queen-size log bed and the feel of a sportsman's lodge. If you like more
traditional furnishings, you'll love the English Garden Room and, my
favorite, cozy Sara's Room under the gables. You'll find great photos of
all the rooms on the inn's website.

Mike is breakfast king, and he serves a hot feast every morning. If
you're in town on business, you'll appreciate that he starts at 7:00 a.m.
on weekdays. Made-to-order eggs are his specialty, and they'll be paired
with options such as Lori's "best ever" waffles or French toast. Guests
dine in the back two rooms, which have large brick fireplaces and the
congenial feeling of a vintage farmhouse. This part of the inn remains
undated, although Mike tells me some of what he has been told: the
beams came from a church, the bricks came from a jail, and the doors
came from a brothel. He laughs and says, "We're well represented!" If
you're partial to primitives, you'll love the long harvest table, which
looks as though it has been there for a hundred years.

The Venturinis love to host special events. They schedule Murder
Mystery Dinners throughout the year, and their Foodie Weekends have
become favorites for guests who like to cook. Mike and Lori furnish all
the food, recipes and directions for making a fabulous Saturday night
supper. Big fun!

If you're thinking of getting married or renewing your vows, ask
about the Thousand Dollar Wedding package. It includes your ceremony, complete with flowers for the bride and groom, a reception and
wedding cake at the inn for up to twenty people and two nights' lodging.
For you're-worth-it pampering, schedule a package of spa services that
can include manicures, pedicures, facials, massages, a variety of exotic
body wraps and waxing for up to fourteen people. Lori is a licensed cos-
metologist, and she works with a team of professionals who come to
the inn.

The Munro House is a great place for parents to stay while visiting
children attending Hillsdale College and all the "camps" they hold on
campus during the year. Antique lovers have a special fondness for this
area. Jonesville is in the heart of "Antique Alley," and the little town
of Allen, known to many as Michigan's antique capital, is just 5 miles
up the road.

Vitals

rooms: 7 with private baths

pets permitted: no

pets in residence: one delightful Scottie named Ozzie

open season: year-round

rates: $99 to $199

e-mail: mike@munrohouse.com

website: www.munrohouse.com

owners/innkeepers:
Lori and Mike Venturini
202 Maumee Street
Jonesville, MI 49250
517-849-9292
800-320-3792

JUGVILLE (WHITE CLOUD)

The Shack

The last time I wrote about The Shack, it was the mid-1980s and this family-owned inn offered six guest rooms. Apparently I wasn't the only one who liked it. It grew in popularity, and it also grew in size—to forty-four rooms!

Owners Janette and Marv Deur were both born and raised within 10 miles of The Shack, but they knew little about it. The name, by the way, is taken from a structure built there in the early 1900s, called the Shack, which burned in 1937. It was replaced with a log lodge constructed by a furniture dealer from Grand Rapids who kept the name. And so did the Deurs when they bought the lodge in 1976. They began taking in guests in 1978 and eleven years later added a large dining room, twenty more sleeping rooms and two conference rooms. There were more renovations in 1992 and many more expansions. The Granary, with eight rooms, and the Livery, with ten rooms, were added across from the lodge, along with a covered recreation area called the O'Hay Corral. There is also a museum, which displays a fascinating collection of early-twentieth-century farm implements and kitchen equipment, Model Ts, small steam engines and vintage Lincoln Continentals.

And if it sounds like the place might be getting a bit crowded, I can assure you it is not. It's all tucked amid 100 acres of woods and meadows along the shore of beautiful Robinson Lake. It's peaceful as can be—a place where you can put your feet up and relax in a log Adirondack-style chair overlooking the lake or walk the trails that course through the property, unwind in your private hot tub or in front of a fireplace, meditate, unplug.

The lodge is the hub of the inn, and it is a grand two-story structure constructed of smooth-peeled logs with cupolas and a portico. It has a two-story wing of guest rooms plus two dining rooms, including one with a soaring two-story vaulted ceiling and large windows that over-

look the lake. Nearly everything in it is constructed of logs or gleaming varnished knotty pine. It is decorated with wildlife prints and collections of antique crocks—this is Jugville, after all! On the walls and in display areas are mounts of deer and antelope, an elk and bison, Michigan mammals and ducks. Indoor shuffleboard courts and billiard tables are on the lower level, as are two large conference rooms that will hold a hundred people.

All forty-four rooms are decorated individually. In the Lodge, you can take your pick from pretty rooms with queen-size beds facing away from the lake and lake-view rooms with whirlpool tubs or two queen beds. When the Deurs designed the large guest rooms in the Granary and the Livery, they added hot tubs and fireplaces to several. Many have full-log walls, log beds, and kitchenettes. And you'll find an abundance of gathering rooms and sitting areas in all the buildings. I met several women who were at The Shack for their annual weekend quilting retreat, as they have been for years, and they were delighted with the large room off the O'Hay Corral where they spread out their projects and quilted for two days straight! Even when The Shack is full, you'll find there are plenty of quiet, out-of-the-way places where you can pass the time.

A buffet breakfast is included with your lodging, and it's hearty country fare: eggs and bacon or sausage, toast and baked goods, plus juice and beverages. Sometimes it includes pancakes or French toast and maple syrup made in The Shack's sugar bush.

Guests staying on Friday or Saturday night are also treated to a buffet supper with country specialties such as baked chicken, baked fish and pot roast; potatoes and vegetables; broccoli slaw salad; and The Shack's special bread pudding. Dinner is open to the public, too, by reservation, as is the Sunday brunch. If you're spending the night, save room for a bedtime banana split. The fixings are brought out just before 9:00 p.m., as they have been since the tradition began in 1978.

Walking the acreage here is a treat. I love the large pavilion that sits at the water's edge and the covered bridge that spans a small creek. In summer the grounds have beautiful flower gardens and hanging baskets. When we visited on a warm, sunny fall day, the lake was still as glass and the trees were glowing red and yellow. It's a setting that invites you to slow down, hold hands and breath in the fresh air. There is plenty of room to picnic and play games on the lawn, and there are paddleboats for guests' use. Two golf courses are nearby. The little town of Jugville has pretty much disappeared, and White Cloud, which is The Shack's mailing address, is just six miles away.

If you plan a spring visit, you may want to time your stay to coincide with the sugar bush. The Deurs produce about 60 gallons of maple syrup here during a good season, and you're welcome to help carry the sap buckets. It's an exhilarating springtime tradition and a lot of fun. If you come in the winter, bring your cross-country skis and snowshoes.

While all this sounds like a great place to bring kids, the Deurs do

not encourage them. They prefer to keep the inn a peaceful respite for adults, and in each building you'll see friendly signs reminding you that 10:30 p.m. is the beginning of quiet time.

The Deurs' strong Christian faith and warm hospitality mingle comfortably here. There is an open-air chapel with a lighted cross that faces the lake and a small prayer pavilion where you'll always find a Bible or two. Our table had a little sign letting us know that Thanksgiving prayer was welcome. There was an open Bible at the registration counter and books on faith and religion in the gift shop. The Shack is well suited to hosting large groups for conferences and retreats, and it is a favorite for faith-based gatherings.

Vitals

rooms: 44 with private baths

pets permitted: no

pets in residence: none

open season: year-round

rates: $65 to $170

e-mail: none, please call

website: www.theshackbandb.com

owners/innkeepers:
  Janette and Marv Deur
  2263 W. 14th Street
  White Cloud, MI 49349
  231-924-6683

KALAMAZOO

Kalamazoo House
Bed and Breakfast

Downtown Kalamazoo was peppered with grand Victorian homes at the end of the nineteenth century. The town was prospering, and couples like David and Emily Lilienfeld looked forward to a stylish life with their young son and daughter when they built their three-story mansion on West South Street in 1878. David had come from Germany. He and Emily were founding members of the Kalamazoo synagogue, and David and his brother started a cigar-making company, which became the largest of about twenty in Kalamazoo. Their advertising slogan was "If you crave a bad cigar, don't smoke Lilies."

Cigar-making businesses thrived here for more than two decades, but they began to dissolve in 1908 when workers tried to unionize. Frustrated company owners simply packed up and moved their companies to other cities with bigger immigrant populations from which they could draw new workers.

For nearly fifty years, the mansion was a single-family home for wealthy industrialists. From the 1920s to the 1970s, it was a funeral home, whose operators raised their family in the rooms on the second floor. When "modernization" efforts crashed through downtown Kalamazoo, devouring historic architecture block by block, the home was scheduled for demolition so the space could be used for parking.

Fortunately, one determined couple, who had already saved several historic buildings, convinced the city that this house should be saved, too. And save it they did. They hired artists to do faux graining on the parlor doors and intricate stenciling in some of the sleeping rooms. They installed Lincrusta embossed wall coverings and Bradbury and Bradbury period-design wallpapers. And they added modern comforts— private baths, zoned heat, central air and, in time, a huge commercial

Preserving the past for the present

Laurel and Terry were thrilled to get a call from one of the Lilienfelds' great-great-great-granddaughters. Not long after that, they got a call from a great-great-grandson of David Lilienfeld's brother. The two families did not know each other, and Laurel was able to put them together. If the Lilienfeld house had been torn down as scheduled, those families might never have met.

Laurel says when you save an old house like the Kalamazoo House, you save more than a building. You preserve a tangible link to the past. You create a place where people can come together. Visitors get an up-close opportunity to explore a city and live, for the moment, in the luxury of another era. You generate business for downtown restaurants, shops and cultural events, and you help keep that city's urban core vibrant.

Oh yes . . . and you give travelers a truly wonderful place in which to work, rest and play.

---

kitchen. They opened for bed-and-breakfast lodging and christened their rescued beauty the Kalamazoo House. If you have visited there, you may remember a restaurant they later opened on the first floor called Lilies.

Fast forward several years. Laurel and Terry Parrott were looking for a new life, and they liked the idea of owning a resort or an inn on water. Yes, definitely a resort sort of place. Certainly in a resort area. And definitely on water.

So why in the world, wondered Laurel, would her broker suggest she check out an inn in the heart of downtown Kalamazoo?

"Just go look at it," he told her. So she did. And she loved what she saw: a spectacular Victorian era urban inn in the midst of a vibrant city, renovated with great care to showcase the sweeping 12 1/2 foot ceilings, three floors of original woodwork and hardware, beautiful fireplaces and a stunning crystal chandelier. The restaurant was closed, but there was still that amazing kitchen and room reservations on the books. She and Terry bought the Kalamazoo House in 2007—turnkey. Laurel remembers that they took possession of it on a Wednesday and had a full house to check in on Friday. And as little miracles sometimes happen, one of the guests that first weekend had grown up in the house. He was the son of the funeral director, and he was back with his best friends to attend their fortieth high school reunion.

The inn is furnished with antiques, reproductions and contemporary pieces chosen as much for their beauty and style as for their comfort. After a long day of driving, I was delighted to arrive in time for welcoming cheese and crackers. Then I sank into an ample wingback chair in the massive living room and took in the grandeur that was typical of homes throughout this neighborhood 125 years ago.

I love the "social hour" tradition that many innkeepers offer. At the Kalamazoo House, it's from 5:30 to 6:30 p.m., and it gave me the opportunity to talk with the innkeepers and several guests. Our eclectic mix of travelers that evening included five women who had graduated from high school in "Kazoo" and were having a reunion, a couple researching brewpubs, and a couple from out of state who had come to Kalamazoo to attended a concert.

Sleeping rooms are located on the second and third floors and are all beautifully decorated and luxurious. Some are spacious suites with whirlpool tubs. Others are smaller and offer tucked-under-the-gables coziness. Five rooms have electric fireplaces. You'll find excellent photos of all of them on the inn's website, so you can choose ahead of your arrival if you like. And do ask about the sheets. They are soft as whipped cream. The Parrotts stock them, and you can buy a set to take home.

There's another sweet tradition here—guests are offered chocolate chip cookies and milk at bedtime.

Terry is the breakfast cook, and he turns out great food. He and Laurel post a menu so each guest can select an entrée for the following morning. I chose the gluten-free, crustless quiche with spinach and feta, which was served with fresh fruit and juice. Other options that morning included banana-nut-crunch or cinnamon-raisin-bread French toast, omelets, Cajun corned beef hash and a frittata. The tables are set for two or four people, so you get the best of both options—privacy if you prefer, or you can join other guests for conversation. And the sun-drenched breakfast room is a lovely place to begin your day.

The Kalamazoo House is located next to the Kalamazoo Institute of Arts and half a block from the Kalamazoo Civic Theater and Bronson Park. Three blocks up the street is Kalamazoo's pedestrian mall with its hip restaurants, taverns, live theater and brewpubs. Kalamazoo College and parts of Western Michigan University are also within walking distance.

So . . . why in the world would you stay at an inn in the heart of Kalamazoo? Now you know!

Vitals

rooms: 10 on the second and third floors, all with private baths

pets permitted: no

pets in residence: none

open season: year-round

rates: $119 to $199

e-mail: thekalamazoohouse@msn.com

website: www.thekalamazoohouse.com

owners/innkeepers:
Laurel and Terry Parrott
447 W. South Street
Kalamazoo, MI 49007
269-382-0880

MARSHALL

The National House Inn

Marshall is a history-lover's paradise. It was designated a National Historic Landmark in 1991, and with more than 850 homes and businesses, it's the largest historic district in Michigan. The National House Inn is located in the heart of this historical mecca, across from Fountain Circle and the white-pillared Brooks Fountain. The inn first opened its doors as a stagecoach stop in 1835 when Michigan was largely unsettled territory and two years from attaining statehood!

Like so many old buildings, this one suffered through various uses as stagecoaches disappeared and the decades passed. Its salvation came in 1976 when new visionary owners carried out a splendid renovation, reclaiming it as an inn once again with modern comforts and loads of early-nineteenth-century charm. When you settle into a Windsor chair beside the massive beam-and-brick hearth on a chilly night or walk through the quiet garden on its brick-paved paths, it's easy to imagine how grateful those first road-weary travelers must have been when their stagecoach came to a stop here.

The inn's fifteen guest rooms have been decorated with period furnishings that feel so appropriate one might imagine that little has changed here in 150 years. Each is named for one of Marshall's early residents, and they vary from the elegant Victorian-style, two-room Ketchum Suite to the petite Andrew Mann Room with country decor and a double walnut bed.

Innkeeper Barbara Bradley says this is where the fast lane ends, and she ought to know. She has been hosting guests here since 1982. And if, indeed, relaxing is high on your list of priorities, you'll find the inn and its lovely parlors are perfect for winding down. Tea and sweets are served in the afternoon. It's such a lovely custom, and in the summer taking tea in the garden is a special pleasure. In the morning you'll enjoy a breakfast feast with items such as baked egg dishes, waffles and

A city rallies

In 1843 slave Adam Crosswhite and his family ran away from Francis Giltner's plantation near Carrollton, Kentucky, after Adam learned that his four children were going to be sold. The family made the difficult trek north, all the way to Marshall, and decided to settle there. When the Giltners heard of their location, Francis organized a group of men, led by his son David, who headed to Marshall to capture and bring back what they believed was their "property."

On January 2, 1847, Giltner's men and a local deputy sheriff began pounding on the Crosswhites' door. Neighbors heard the noise and came running. They yelled "slave catchers!" through the streets of town, and more than one hundred people surrounded the home in support of Adam and his family.

One of Giltner's men demanded that people in the crowd give him their names, which they did, proudly. They even shouted out the correct spelling. The deputy sheriff, apparently swayed by the crowd's intent, decided he should arrest the "slave catchers." By the time bond was posted, the Crosswhites were on their way to Canada.

In Federal Court in Detroit, the Giltners sued for damages the townspeople whose names they had collected. Many were fined, and, the story goes, they paid up, as they considered the fine a badge of honor.

Because of this event and others like it, in 1850 Kentucky senator Henry Clay pushed through Congress the Fugitive Slave Act, which made it very risky to help an escaped slave.

The National House Inn has a beautiful country-style room named in honor of Adam Crosswhite.

---

pastries—plenty to get you started on your day. And without even getting back in your car, your day can include shopping and visiting the many restaurants, historic buildings and museums within walking distance of the inn. Make your first stop the Tin Whistle Gift Shop right in the inn, next to the dining room. It's stocked with a mix of antiques and country-themed gifts and is the perfect place to find treasures for friends and family back home.

The inn offers a popular package that combines lodging with dinner at nearby Schuler's Restaurant and a tour of the Honolulu House Museum. There are also tours of historic buildings and gardens scheduled throughout the year. The Christmas Candlelight Tour takes small groups inside several of the area's homes when they are decorated for

Christmas and lit by candlelight. It's quite a moving experience and may be as close as you'll come to understanding what life was like in Marshall when stagecoaches passed through regularly bringing news and visitors from Detroit and Chicago.

Vitals

rooms: 15 with private baths

pets permitted: no

pets in residence: none

open season: year-round

rates: $120 to $170

e-mail: frontdesk@nationalhouseinn.com

website: www.nationalhouseinn.com

innkeeper:
Barbara Bradley
102 South Parkview
Marshall, MI 49068
269-781-7374

MOUNT PLEASANT

Country Chalet and Edelweiss Haus

If you've ever traveled to another country and fallen in love with the architecture and lifestyle, you'll understand why there is an authentic Bavarian-style guest house perched on 25 rolling and wooded acres just northwest of Mount Pleasant.

Carolyn and Ron Lutz were both teachers, and early in their careers Ron accepted an offer to teach at the American Dependent Schools in Kaiserslautern, Germany. The town has about one hundred thousand residents, a huge percentage of whom are North Atlantic Treaty Organization (NATO) military personnel. Between 1950 and 1955, Kaiserslautern developed into the largest US military community outside the United States.

The Lutzes had two young children at the time, and when Ron got home from teaching on Friday afternoon, he and Carolyn and the kids would hop into the car and head out to explore Europe. "When we went to Italy for the first time, we passed through Austria," remembers Ron. "We were fascinated by the peaceful nature of the Austrian people, and by the gorgeous scenery." Those images stuck. When they returned to Michigan, they decided to build a home that embodied many of the things they loved about their travels to Austria and the Bavarian regions of Germany. They completed their Country Chalet in 1972 and raised six children there.

By the late 1990s, the children were grown and on their own, and Carolyn and Ron began looking at options for retirement.

They had been close friends for decades with Ron Gibson, owner and innkeeper of the Victorian Villa in Union City. Ron Gibson had done his student teaching under Ron Lutz's supervision. So when Ron Gibson suggested they consider becoming innkeepers . . . well . . . that

was a pretty interesting idea. Around the same time, a friend showed the Lutzes a picture of a Bavarian-style home he hoped to build. Ron and Carolyn loved it. Ron built a model of it. Then he built the real thing—with a little help from friends and former students—just down the hill from their Country Chalet. It had all the Austrian, Swiss and German touches they had come to love, and they named it Edelweiss Haus. They opened for bed-and-breakfast guests in 2000.

If you've been similarly captivated by Bavarian architecture and the gentle way of life in that region, this will all look and feel wonderfully familiar to you. From the wraparound balconies and lush flower boxes outside to the hand-built wooden dining table and benches, collections of Bavarian memorabilia and down comforters on the beds, it's Old World Europe with modern conveniences and a few new twists.

"We're addicted to self-sufficiency!," Ron says with a smile. When the children were young, the family had a milk cow and chickens and other farm animals. These days Carolyn, who is a master gardener, tends a large garden and an orchard from which they get nearly half the food they make for their guests, including juices and jams. The cleaning products they use are ecofriendly, and they recycle and compost. Hot water for showers and laundry is heated by solar panels, and if you visit the inn in chilly weather, you'll love the European-style heated floors.

Each of the four guest rooms has a door to the balconies and great

A musical family

Carolyn and Ron talked to their son Jim about a piece of music they wanted as background on their website, but he felt it would be expensive to obtain the rights to use it. So he wrote a piece just for them, and it's lovely. Do check it out. Ron says the whole family is musical, and Jim is musical director for Cirque du Soleil Kooza!

views of the rolling countryside. They also have TVs, housed in armoires, so guests can ignore them completely if they wish. Some B&Bs are not suited to the needs of children, but Carolyn and Ron welcome them here. The 25 acres offer plenty of room for running and playing, and there are two ponds stocked with fish that children can feed from a bridge. A closet full of toys and games helps provide entertainment if the weather turns disagreeable.

The Country Chalet is just beyond the Edelweiss Haus and can be rented as a three-bedroom, one-bath suite for groups or families traveling together. There's a large common area and a deck that overlooks the woods. "We watch the seasons change here," says Carolyn. "Every season has something special to offer."

When not exploring outside or bird-watching, guests staying in both houses love to gather in the first-floor great room in the Edelweiss Haus to eat (Carolyn makes great dried-cherry oatmeal cookies!) and tell stories. Often their guests have come to the Mount Pleasant area to see friends and family—especially parents of students attending Central Michigan University. Many have become good friends, and that's a big part of what Ron and Carolyn love about running the inn. "Caroline and I were both teachers, and we had close relationships with our students," says Ron. "This is a wonderful extension of that . . . without having to grade papers!"

Breakfast is served family style, and it's hearty! You'll start with good German coffee and homemade juices. There's always a large platter of fresh fruit, dishes such as a layered stove-top potato and vegetable strata, eggs and heart-shaped waffles with a homemade fruit topping. You might also be treated to Carolyn's blueberry pancakes, which Ron says are "the best pancakes in the world!" Breads and parfaits with fruit and yogurt are often on the menu, too. Breakfast is usually served between 8:00 and 10:00 a.m., depending on each guest's preference.

I'm not going to get to Bavaria this year, but the afternoon I spent at

the Edelweiss Haus filled me up and made me feel as though I'd been there.

Vitals

rooms: 4 in the Edelweiss Haus with private baths, 3 in the Country Chalet that share 1 bath

pets permitted: no

pets in residence: none

open season: year-round

rates: $99 to $129

e-mail: RCL9259@earthlink.net

website: www.countrychalet.net

owners/innkeepers:
Carolyn and Ron Lutz
723 S. Meridian Road
Mount Pleasant, MI 48858
989-772-9259

MOUNT PLEASANT

Ginkgo Tree Inn

Oh, how I love it when a fine old home with a bit of history and a lot of charm is saved from demolition!

A surgeon named Dr. Gardiner began building this home in 1902, and, as the legend goes, he took his time because he was also looking for a wife. Once he met his bride to be, he quickly finished what had become a three-year project, and it became both the Gardiners' home and his offices. When his wife died, he married his niece so the home could stay in the family. And indeed, the family owned it until the 1960s, when Verda Marie Davis bought it. As the new owner, she suffered some teasing. Why, people asked, would a "spinster" want such a large home? But Verda Marie loved to have company and feed her guests. She eventually married a Mr. Gwaltney, who was an architect, and after he passed away she rented parts of the house to students.

"This house was made to be an inn," says Jean Prout, recalling Verda Marie's hospitality with a smile. Jean purchased it from the City of Mount Pleasant, which had acquired the house when Verda Marie died in 2005. It had been empty for a few years, and it needed a lot of help. Despite its forlorn condition, Jean completed an astounding renovation in less than a year. Nearly everything is new except the decorative wood trim around the windows, sets of pocket doors and the striking open stairway you see when you first enter. Jean also added an eye-catching two-story turret that blends in so seamlessly I assumed it was original to the home. She named her inn after the ginkgo trees in the backyard, and she likes the fact that two previous owners' names began with *G* as well.

The first floor of the home is now the Riverbluff Bistro which serves lunch daily in three elegant rooms and on the front veranda and back patio. The tables and chairs inside are antique oak, and each is set with

Photo by Spinning Lens Photography, courtesy of Ginko Tree Inn

a white tablecloth and a vase of fresh flowers. Victorian-style wall coverings create an opulent backdrop.

Jean's menu includes traditional salads, sandwiches and soups, turned up a notch. For example, the pear and cherry salad is tossed with toasted pecans and served with a champagne vinaigrette. The spinach salad is topped with blueberries, pecans, bacon, bleu cheese and red onion. There's a fragrant three-cheese onion au gratin soup, and the open-faced Maryland-style crab cakes are served on warmed English muffins with parmesan cheese and a special house sauce. If you saved room, take a look at the dessert menu and consider, perhaps, a slice of Kentucky bourbon pecan pie or—one of my favorites—an old-fashioned lemon bar.

There are five stunning guest rooms on the second and third floors furnished with fine antiques and reproductions and decorated with luxurious fabrics and Victorian-style wall coverings. The petite Lincoln Library is adjacent to the Sugarplum Room and has a connecting door so the two rooms can be rented together as a suite. When not rented, the library is open for all overnight guests to use. The Grand Ginkgo Room has one of the home's original fireplaces. The Golden Oak Room includes the second-floor turret, which is a cozy sitting room with a

Locks of love

Jean visited Germany in 2012 and discovered bridges that were laden with beautiful locks. She learned that in the early 1900s, as people went off to war, they put their initials on a lock and affixed it to the bridge.

She was captivated by the image and the symbolism. Realizing that the Ginkgo Tree Inn sits on a river and has a metal fence, she started a tradition for couples getting married there. At the end of their ceremony, they put their lock on the fence and throw the key into the river. Then they kiss and are pronounced husband and wife. "It signifies that their love is locked, and since the key is thrown away, no one can break them apart," says Jean. "People clap and cry, and it's a lot of fun!"

Guests who come to celebrate their anniversary at the inn are also invited to bring a lock for the fence and date it with their wedding day. By the end of the summer of 2012, there were already six locks on the fence.

---

fireplace and a Victorian couch and chairs. In the tradition of Victorian homes at the turn of the century, some of the rooms have antique Asian furniture and accessories. For the Victorians, having things that came from the Orient was a sign of status and an indication of wealth because shipping goods from there to the United States was expensive!

Jean put all the main lights in the rooms on dimmers, which puzzled her electrician and delights her guests. Do take a moment to look at the Italian chandelier above the landing on the third floor. Oh my!

Breakfast for overnight guests is a four-course, chef-prepared feast with great beginnings such as egg dishes, stuffed French toast and fresh fruit with yogurt. For those who prefer them, there are vegan, vegetarian, gluten-free and sugar-free items to choose from as well.

"Every day is perfect if you start it with chocolate and wine," Jean says, "So we serve both together—a chocolate wine produced by a Dutch company." This makes me laugh. I was raised on the southeast side of Grand Rapids, which was pretty solidly Dutch when I was growing up. Why have I never heard of this heavenly concoction?

Although the Ginkgo Tree Inn is not officially open for breakfast, when Jean is cooking for overnight guests she opens for the public, too. Locals know to call and ask, and Jean says the inn is getting so busy that she's serving breakfast nearly every weekend and many weekdays now. Lucky locals!

When I visited the inn in September, I got a sneak preview of Jean's current project. She purchased the house next door, which was built in the 1890s, and is creating Chateau Riviera, which will have four sleeping rooms, including two on the first floor. Check the Ginkgo Tree's website for updates.

The Ginkgo Tree Inn is wonderfully suited to hosting weddings and special occasions. Tents are available for outdoor events, and plans call for creating a bar in the vintage building behind the inn, where views of the river and its tiny island are nearly unobstructed in the winter. Jean retired from teaching hospitality services at Central Michigan University, and she is clearly having a great time creating lovely venues for lodging, food and fun around the Ginkgo Tree Inn.

Vitals

rooms: 6 in the Ginkgo Tree Inn, 5 with private baths. The 6th room is a library connected to the Sugarplum Room and can be rented with it. Chateau Riviera will have 4 rooms, 2 with private baths and 2 that share a bath.

pets permitted: welcome in two rooms in Chateau Riviera and must be crated when their owners are not in the room with them.

pets in residence: none

open season: year-round

rates: $99 to $210

e-mail: info@ginkgotreeinn.com

website: www.ginkgotreeinn.com

owner/innkeeper:
Jean Prout
309 N. Main Street
Mount Pleasant, MI 48858
989-773-TREE (8733)

The Victorian Villa Inn

The Victorian Villa Inn has held a special place in my heart, as has Ron Gibson, its owner, since I first visited this magnificent Victorian mansion in the mid-1980s. For romance and Victoriana, it's at the top of my list—a jewel where you go to imbibe the gentle side of life.

Ron might possibly have been happier born in the nineteenth century when Victoriana was coming into vogue, but he's done the next best thing. He has brought it back to life for the last forty years to the delight of thousands of guests, editors at the former *Victoria* magazine, *Wine Spectator*, the *Malt Advocate* and scores of travel writers. From the moment you walk in the door—actually, as soon as you stroll across the lawn amid Victorian-style gardens and those lush ferns that the Victorians were so crazy about, you know that someone has turned back the clock.

This majestic home was built by Dr. William P. Hurd and his wife Caroline in 1876 at a cost of about $12,000—a tiny sum, it seems, until you realize that the craftspeople who worked on it made as little as eight cents a day. Dr. Hurd became founder and chairman of the National Bank of Union City. He helped the town grow and prosper, and he brought a lot of its babies into the world. Residents loved him. But only five years after moving into his villa, Dr. Hurd died. Caroline remained in the home until 1910. By 1950 this glorious mansion was going the way of so many huge old homes—it was converted to apartments.

It is impossible to envision this place as it was when Ron bought it because the restoration of its opulence is seamless and complete. Fireplaces were repaired, wooden shutters were replaced, gardens were planted. Carefully selecting each piece, Ron filled the rooms with the oil paintings, parlor plants, antique bedsteads, glass lamps and lace and finery that the Victorians loved. And the high quality of the workman-

ship built into this fine home shines through. As you can imagine, this is the perfect place to hold an old-fashioned Victorian wedding.

The ten bedchambers and suites located in the main home and the adjacent Carriage House are furnished with all the styles of the Victorian era, from 1850s empire, through renaissance and eastlake to the art nouveau look of the 1890s. Memorabilia in the Dr. Watson bedchamber evokes a feeling that Ron refers to as "gaslight London." The elaborately carved, museum-quality bedsteads in the Victorian Master Suite and the Victorian Renaissance Suite date to the 1870s, and both have headboards more than 8 feet tall. Each bedchamber has a private bath, and some have soaking tubs rather than showers. Two rooms have private baths that are not attached.

Do take the stairs to the third floor, where there are two cozy under-the-eves bedchambers and a small sitting room with a stairway that leads to the widow's walk. Every time I look out those windows, I expect to see ladies in long dresses sipping tea in the garden and a horse-drawn carriage coming up the street.

A very nice breakfast is available each morning, and it's a little more elaborate on Saturday and Sunday. If you really want to settle in and enjoy all that this lovely inn has to offer, consider adding a reservation for a petite afternoon tea, served from 3:00 to 4:00 p.m., and a wine tasting from 4:00 to 5:00. Over the years Ron has built a well-deserved reputation for serving fine food at the inn. His intimate Victoria's Restaurant on the first floor serves a seven-course champagne dinner on Saturday evenings that is open to guests and the public, and sometimes you'll be joined by one of Ron's close friends: General George Armstrong Custer, Mark Twain, Charles Dickens or Sherlock Holmes. Seatings are at 6:00 and 7:00 p.m., and reservations are required twenty-four hours in advance.

If you like Scotch . . . this is the place to come. "I knew I was Irish on one side, and then I learned that the other side of my family was from Scotland," says Ron. "I wanted to know more about the country and about single-malt Scotch." If there's one thing I know about Ron, when he's interested in something, he does it big, which is why he now has what looks like the largest collection of single-malt Scotch whiskies outside of Scotland. Ok . . . that may be a bit of an exaggeration, but you get my point. For Scotch enthusiasts, he holds a Single-Malt Scotch and Cigar-Tasting Event and Dinner during which you get to sample single-malt Scotch whiskies and enjoy nineteenth-century Scottish cuisine—yes, haggis, too. Be brave.

Call or check the website to learn about all the other theme events Ron holds during the year. I was able to show off my acting skills when I attended a Sherlock Holmes mystery weekend and helped figure out "who done it." Each guest had a role in the plot, and as a femme fatale I took great delight in my stage direction, which instructed me to "faint on the staircase!"

My favorites of all the activities at the Villa are the Old-Fashioned Christmas weekends held in December. The Victorians loved Christmas, and from your arrival on Friday until you depart on Sunday, you will be surrounded by sparkling trees and mistletoe, ribbons and garlands, angels and ornaments. You'll enjoy high tea, parlor magic and sumptuous meals, including a traditional holiday feast on Saturday evening. Charles Dickens himself will pay a visit and read aloud the beloved story *A Christmas Carol.* These weekends have become so popular that guests sometimes book a reservation two years in advance. If you are looking for a very special way to usher in the holidays, this is it.

There are shops and festivals and a wealth of country pleasures to enjoy within an easy drive of the Villa. If you want to re-create the beauty of Victorian lighting in your own home, stop at Ron's shop in Union City, the 19th Century Lighting Company. It specializes in museum replica Tiffany lighting—table lamps and pendants—plus stained-glass windows. It has a website where you can order these beauties, along with Ron's book, *19th Century Patterned Art-Glass Chamber Lamps.* And before you leave town, stop at Ron's latest venture, a friendly coffee shop called The Daily Grind, with great baked goods, wonderful coffee and a good-looking menu.

Vitals

rooms: 10 in the main home and Carriage House with private baths.

pets permitted: no

pets in residence: none

open season: year-round

rates: $85 to $160

e-mail: info@avictorianvilla.com

website: www.avictorianvilla.com

owner: Ron Gibson

innkeeper:
Cynthia Shattuck
601 N. Broadway St.
Union City, MI 49094
517-741-7383
800-348-4552 (800-34-VILLA)

SOUTHERN SUNRISE: THE SOUTHEASTERN LOWER PENINSULA

Auburn Hills
  Cobblestone Manor

Bay City
  Chesny's Keswick Manor
  The Historic Webster House

Lexington
  A Night to Remember Bed and Breakfast

Plymouth
  932 Penniman

Ypsilanti
  The Parish House Inn

AUBURN HILLS

Cobblestone Manor

If Cobblestone Manor could talk, oh the stories it could tell . . .

Nathan G. Terry built the earliest part of this home in 1840, just three years after Michigan became a state. It was a large manor with eleven rooms and roughly 3,200 square feet of nineteenth-century comfort. Nathan was a successful farmer, and he grew his landholdings to 340 acres. An agriculture report issued in 1872 rated his operation an "A Number 1" farm.

In 1916 much of the farmland was sold to Matilda Dodge Wilson, who added it to the substantial number of adjacent acres she already owned. She cofounded the Oakland campus of Michigan State University, now Oakland University, on her 1,400-acre estate called Meadow Brook Farms, and part of that land included acreage purchased from the Terry farm.

The manor fell on hard times and was abandoned for a time during the Depression. When it was finally purchased, it was renovated and converted to three very nice apartments. And that's the way it stayed for decades.

Heather and Paul Crandall love restoring old buildings, and the home turned apartment building had a lot of appeal. They bought it in 1994, fully intending to keep it as apartments. Then they got calls from developers who wanted to buy it—just for the 2 acres of land on which it now sits. The Crandalls knew that meant the 150-year-old building would be torn down, slate roof and all. So they looked at other options for its use, and they decided it was perfectly suited, and perfectly located, to be a bed and breakfast. It was their ninth historic home project, and they started by learning all they could about B&B lodging and the tastes of today's travelers.

"We wanted to create an excellent ambiance and a feel of history, and to have contemporary luxuries such as whirlpool tubs, granite

bathrooms and fireplaces," says Paul, who was delighted to have places to put the antiques and other treasures that he and Heather had been collecting since they got married. And after adding 5,500 square feet to the original home and designing nine guest rooms and suites, there were plenty of places to put them! They added period wallpapers and fine reproduction beds, including many classic four-posters. Some of the rooms have private parlors or sitting areas, and several have arched windows and walls and ceilings that follow the curved lines of the mansard roof.

One of Heather's favorite rooms is the Meadowlark Suite, which you enter through leaded-glass French doors. It has everything you need for privacy and luxury, including a parlor with a fireplace and a sleeping room with a massive king-size mahogany bed, marble-topped bedside tables and a six-foot whirlpool tub. Oh yes, the countertop in the bathroom is granite. When we talked on a crisp fall day, Heather and Paul were excited about antique plaster pillars they acquired in Detroit and had recently installed around the tub. "They have marble bases and beautiful capitals," Heather explained. "They make the tub look like a Roman spa!"

The Presidential Suite, with its king-size bed draped in yards of gorgeous fabric, is the Manor's crowning jewel. Adjacent to the bedroom is a library with a fireplace flanked by two recliners, and a desk from Henry Ford's Fairlane Estate. The bathroom is granite, and it has a large whirlpool tub plus a big steam shower. From the doors of the "false balcony," guests have a bird's-eye view of the lovely wedding garden below.

There is a lovely living room on the first floor for guests' use. A spiral staircase takes you to the lower level where there is another beautiful sitting room. In good weather you'll likely find guests relaxing in the screened gazebo, too.

"We are in automation alley," says Paul, explaining that Auburn Hills now has the third-largest number of employees in the state. Several automotive-related companies and offices for innovative corporations are in the area. Both the Chrysler Technical Center and Volkswagen headquarters are nearby.

Given that location, breakfast has been thoughtfully arranged to suit the needs of both business guests and those on vacation. On weekdays it's available beginning at 7:30 a.m. On weekends guests may choose to be served at either 9:30 or 10:00. Every day the elegant meal includes a mixed fruit selection, a breakfast meat and an entrée that alternates between savory and sweet. Orange croissant French toast with orange honey syrup is a house specialty, along with an asparagus and leek crustless quiche and blueberry-stuffed French toast. Guests also love the hot chili-cheese egg puff, which is served with sides of guacamole, sour cream, sweet salsa, and cornbread. If you need to depart early or you like lighter fare, there's a self-serve breakfast with fresh fruit, muffins or toast, juice and coffee. Heather says business travelers sometimes leave for their early meetings and return in time to eat a full breakfast!

Brides love the Manor, and the Crandalls have hosted many wedding ceremonies. The 2 acres of grounds, wedding garden and white pergola are picturesque and private. The area can comfortably accommodate fifty guests plus the wedding party. There is also a tented wedding chapel, which extends the outdoor season.

Despite the busy corridor that has grown up around this once pastoral farm, as soon as you step inside the Manor, the noise and busy pace of the outside world drop away. It's quiet, tranquil and luxurious—everything you could want from a historic urban inn.

Vitals

rooms: 9 rooms and suites with private baths

pets permitted: no

pets in residence: 1 cocker spaniel allowed into guest rooms only by special invitation

open season: year-round

rates: $179 to $349

e-mail: stay@cobblestonemanor.com

website: www.cobblestonemanor.com

owners/innkeepers:
Heather and Paul Crandall
3151 University Drive
Auburn Hills, MI 48326
248-370-8000

BAY CITY

Chesney's Keswick Manor

Word around Bay City is that Anna Taylor, who survived going over Niagara Falls in a barrel in 1901, wasn't in just any old barrel. It was a Bousfield barrel from Bay City's Bousfield Woodenware Works, at one time the largest woodenware factory in the country. Robert E. Bousfield, who owned the company with his brother, built this fine home at the end of the nineteenth century. It was designed by an architect who created several other homes in the neighborhood around the same time, including Robert's brother's home. But both houses look different from the others. There's a good reason for that. Rather than going with building trends in Bay City at the time, the brothers took the architect to Chicago and pointed out the styles and features they liked best and wanted in their homes. For Robert it was a mix of colonial revival and neoclassical elements. But his love affair with his house didn't last long. In 1903 he sold it to Frank and Eva Woodworth. Mr. Woodworth made his fortune in lumber and was mayor of Bay City for the first two years he lived here.

A succession of other owners followed—prominent families that were successful in business, and when you see the ionic columns and bay windows, graceful arches and myriad architectural details inside, you will understand what attracted them to this marvelous residence. In 2000 it was turned into a bed-and-breakfast home and named Keswick Manor, after an area in Great Britain that the innkeepers loved.

Graham and Christine Chesny drove by the Manor for three years. They were looking for a change and thought that owning a bed-and-breakfast home might be a good fit for them. "We love to entertain," says Graham, who had a catering business and has been cooking since he was twelve. He also attended a military school, so he learned to be fastidious as well. They fell in love with the house and bought it. Graham left his work as a sound engineer and became an innkeeper. Besides

embarking on a new career, he got a home that's on the Center Avenue Historic District Walking Tour.

Chesny's Keswick Manor is part urban inn, part romantic getaway, and with Graham's skill in the kitchen, it's also a private restaurant just for overnight guests.

"The chef part of this business is my passion," says Graham with enthusiasm. Your first taste of his cooking will be around 6:00 p.m., after you've had time to settle in and unpack and you're ready for a little something to hold you over until you go out for dinner. Graham serves a dessert then, often made with seasonal fruit. When I visited in late summer, he had created a blackberry buckle for guests. Sometimes it's brownies or cookies or European-style pastries.

With twenty-four-hour notice, you can reserve dinner as well, and here's where this creative chef really has fun. Graham loves to make classic French dishes such as roast game hen served in a dijon wine sauce with rice and green beans lyonnaise or coquille saint jacques—sautéed scallops in a wine cream sauce—with mashed redskin potatoes. His tempting menu is on the website. If you're not hungry when you start reading, you will be when you finish. Most of the items include meat. If you prefer a gluten-free, vegan or vegetarian menu, ask Graham about options.

Breakfast is similarly creative. It will likely start with freshly cut fruit and juices and include baked goods and a hot entrée such as German-style pancakes, a Greek quiche with feta and sundried tomatoes or a rosemary potato cake. Graham likes to draw on his Polish roots for specialties, too. If the inn is full, he will set up the meal as a buffet or serve it family style. For small groups, he plates the food. Before it comes out of the kitchen, it's garnished, so it's lovely to look at as well.

"We also cater small events such as showers, small weddings and parties for up to fifty sit-down guests," says Graham. And that has given him the pleasure of being able to open the inn to local residents. For large parties he partners with a banquet chef who was born in Austria and is a former chef at Mackinac Island's Grand Hotel. The Manor's large, open, first-floor rooms work perfectly for gatherings, and its original sconces, chandeliers, corbels and acorn finials almost preclude the need to decorate further!

Guest rooms are on the second floor, and staying true to the style of the house, they have sleek lines and traditional-style furnishings plus luxurious linens. The look is sophisticated and warm, not fussy. The extralarge Bousfield Suite, which was the master bedroom of the origi-

nal owner, has a sitting room with a fireplace and a large private deck. It's perfect if you want to settle in for a few days. The Smith Suite has a separate room with a four-person hot tub! The Chesnys live in the home's adjacent carriage house, so they are never far away if you need something.

I love the surprises here: a cozy library with a coffered ceiling, a sitting room on the second floor where you'll find coffee waiting for you in the morning, French cuisine prepared just for you and served in front of a fireplace, a breakfast room with large windows overlooking perennial gardens. Then there's the gracious veranda across the front of the Manor and the urns full of annuals that Christine creates to complement the classic architecture. I like staying in mansions that are now inns. They give you a closeup look at a time in history when great fortunes were being made, and you get to spend some time in the grand homes those fortunes built.

Vitals

rooms: 4, 3 with private baths. The 4th room is used if it is rented with 1 of the other rooms, with which it would then share a bath.

pets permitted: no

pets in residence: none

open season: year-round

rates: $75 to $190

e-mail: innkeeper@keswickmanor.com

website: www.keswickmanor.com

owners/innkeepers:
Christine and Graham Chesny
1800 Center Avenue
Bay City, MI 48708
989-893-6598

BAY CITY

The Historic Webster House

Judge Thomas E. Webster could be called an early achiever. He was born in 1848 in New York and ran away from home at the age of sixteen to join the Union Army as the Civil War raged. After receiving an honorable discharge, he continued his education, which eventually took him to the University of Michigan. In 1874 Thomas moved to Bay City and began practicing law. He quickly became a man of prominence in the city, and six years later he was elected probate judge for Bay County.

In 1886 he commissioned the building of a majestic Queen Anne home on Fifth Street. The neighborhood was becoming known for spectacular residences, and he and his wife Ella must have believed they would have many happy years there. But tragedy struck. Their life together was cut short when Ella died shortly after childbirth, leaving two young sons. Thomas continued to live in the home, and eventually married Isabel Ingraham, with whom he had a daughter they named Amelia. When Amelia grew up, he built her a lovely home next door, which still stands.

By all accounts, Judge Webster was a compassionate man who never forgot his experiences as a soldier during the war. He organized the Peninsula Military Company of Bay City, which was the city's first organization for war veterans. A notice in the *Bay City Times* dated November 19, 1939, lists him as the last remaining member of the Grand Army of the Republic, also a veterans' organization. He lived to be ninety-two and died in the home he lived in and loved for more than half a century.

Deborah and Steven Ingersoll bought the home in 2009, and although it had been in foreclosure for three years, many of the architectural details such as hand-carved woodwork, fireplaces, pocket doors and original windows were still in place, unharmed. Deborah wanted to recreate the gracious residence it had been when the Websters lived there,

A photo history

Among his many skills, Judge Webster was a photographer whose prints document life in the Bay City area. Deborah purchased several of his photos from the local historical society. They now hang on the walls of the inn so you can get a glimpse, through the judge's lens, of the area and the people who lived there decades ago.

and to open it for bed-and-breakfast guests. When you see it now, it is easy to believe you have opened a door into the early twentieth century.

You'll enter at the side of the house and come into a room with tables set for four, where guests have breakfast. This was the judge's office, conveniently located by that side door so people could come see him without having to go through the entire first floor of the residence.

Beyond the breakfast room are two elegant parlors, with polished oak floors and large, bright window alcoves, and the original formal dining room. Each has ornate woodwork and elegant Victorian-reproduction wallpapers or faux-painted walls with period stenciling.

On the second and third floors are six guest rooms in which Deborah has carried through the same opulent style as the first floor, furnishing them with beautiful bedsteads, luxurious linens and even Asian influences. Victorians loved to include furniture, art and accessories from the Orient. It was a sign of status that they could afford imported goods.

The Signature Room, one of my favorites, pays tribute to the home's original paperhanger, who signed the wall with a flourish in 1888. Rather than covering over this sweet touch of the past, Deborah had that section of the wall framed to preserve it and applied the new wall covering around it. I love it! A stately mantle with an electric fireplace and a table for two in the window alcove complete this fine room.

I was also taken with the Magistrate's Room, located on the third floor under the gables. The bed is set against an original brick hearth and is flanked overhead by two skylights. On a clear night, you can fall asleep looking at the stars.

All the rooms have private baths. Some are marble, and several of the rooms have whirlpool tubs.

A filling, hot breakfast is served on china and with crystal between 8:30 and 9:30 each morning. The formal dining room is not often used, but sometimes when families or groups are traveling together they are seated there so they can eat together.

When you look at the home from the outside, you'll notice that a significant part of the basement is above ground. Still, it was a bit of a surprise when I saw the wide, open stairway leading to the lower level of this home. Finished basements were not popular with the Victorians. The stairs were added by the Ingersolls, who used the ample space in the basement to create a wine cellar and a most amazing spa room.

The wine cellar is at the bottom of the stairs, and it's open to all overnight guests, who enjoy it especially from 5:00 to 6:00 p.m. each evening when innkeepers Gail and Frank Partee hold a wine and cheese reception. Aside from being a very cool room, you get a look at the sturdy foundation that has been supporting this home for 125 years. And the wine cellar is just the start of the fun down here. Beyond it is the spa room with wood and original stone and brick foundation walls, a dry cedar sauna, a large whirlpool tub set into a stone alcove and a rain shower for two. With your lodging you can add a package and reserve this romantic room, complete with heated floors, an electric fireplace, a wine cooler and terry robes, from check-in until 11:00 p.m. You can even arrange ahead of your stay for a massage for two.

You can schedule a massage in your room, as well, and there are different kinds for different situations, including pregnancy massages and body wraps.

Vitals

rooms: 6 with private baths

pets permitted: no

pets in residence: none

open season: year-round

rates: $146 to $196. Spa package is $100

e-mail: info@historicwebsterhouse.com

website: www.historicwebsterhouse.com

owners: Deborah and Steven Ingersoll

innkeepers:
Gail and Frank Partee
900 Fifth Street
Bay City, MI 48708
989-316-2552
877-229-9704

LEXINGTON

A Night to Remember
Bed and Breakfast

This is the perfect place to come if you're looking for antiques and "shabby chic" furniture, decorative garden ironwork, lace and candles and a hot fudge sundae before you settle into your romantic, antique-filled guest room. At first glance the grounds of this bed and breakfast resemble a little village. Separate buildings house an antique shop, a tiny gift store and an ice cream parlor called Temptations. There are gardens galore and containers of colorful annuals, which set off wood-chipped footpaths. A soothing little waterfall flows into a landscaped pond, and when I visited in September, drifts of beautiful black-eyed susans bordered a decorative bridge. Owners Nadine and Dan Maliniak call their little shopping area Marketplace on Main.

The tour de force that brings it all together is an adjacent Italianate brick Victorian mansion, built by a family of blacksmiths in 1870. The house was in rough shape when Nadine and Dan bought it in 2000. It had been empty for a few years, but beyond its neglected state, they could see striking still-intact features—magnificent crystal chandeliers, arched windows plus a sunny bay in the living room, a graceful winding staircase to the second floor and original tile bathrooms for starters. For several years, they operated home decor shops on the first floor and lived on the second.

In 2006 they transferred much of the retail business to the little shops on the grounds and turned five first- and second-floor rooms into opulent guest quarters with private baths. "We invested in great beds," remembers Nadine, "and most of the rest of the furnishings came from our inventory of antiques and shabby chic pieces!"

Each room is loaded with treasures—silk flower garlands, folk art, china cups, lace curtains, floral linens and wallpapers, vintage prints,

From the history books

The first hotel in Lexington was built in 1840, and it was made of logs. It was destroyed by fire in 1859 and rebuilt in 1860. More than 150 years later, it is still standing at the four corners and operates as the Cadillac House Restaurant and Pub. Its ghost's name is George.

The first sawmill was built here in 1846, and three docks were kept busy as lumber and wood products were loaded onto schooners, which transported them to Detroit, Cleveland and Chicago. Wood shingles could be used as currency. They had a value of $1 per thousand, and one thousand shingles bought a barrel of flour. A powerful storm took out all three docks in 1913, and they were never rebuilt. Among the town's notable citizens was Albert Sleeper, who worked in his uncle's store here before he became governor of Michigan in 1920.

pretty lamps, tinware and more. I was smitten with each of them, especially the cheery Garden Room. I slept deeply and peacefully in the Forest Room, which was added to the back of the house in recent years. It offers a more masculine setting with brick and bead board walls, a vaulted knotty pine ceiling, a collection of folk art birdhouses and a private patio with a landscaped sitting area. It's quiet as can be, and the electric fireplace and wingback chairs make it quite cozy. To get to it, you walk through the remaining little shop on the main floor, which displays Heritage Lace and Swan Creek candles. I liked that. You really have to be looking for this room to find it, and it's the most private of the five. The beds are amazing, and guests love the sheets so much that Nadine now sells them in the gift shop.

Breakfast is served in the lovely main floor room in front of a fireplace and under the light of an enormous crystal chandelier. It's an elegant meal with white tablecloths and vintage china. Typically, Nadine serves fresh fruit, a rich egg casserole with potatoes and cheese, a selection of breakfast meats, waffles with strawberries to top them, and a sweet bread. I enjoyed dining with a couple visiting from Switzerland. They had driven through Wisconsin and Michigan and were on their way to Toronto. When I asked why they chose to stay at A Night to Remember, they told me with great enthusiasm that they saw it for the first time when they drove by, and it touched them. I know that feeling.

After you've unpacked, visited all the shops on the property, pol-

ished off a bowl of ice cream and eaten the yummy cookies Nadine will leave for you in your room, do take a look around this sweet town. Lexington was founded in 1835 and was the first settlement on Lake Huron north of Port Huron. As the story goes, Reuben Diamond, an early resident of the village, chose the name Lexington in recognition of his wife's cousin, Ethan Allen, who fought in the Battle of Lexington during the Revolutionary War.

From the inn you can walk the few blocks to Lake Huron and downtown Lexington with its cute shops and markets, a good library, a few places to eat and a collection of very old, well-maintained homes. You'll see lots of white picket fences here, stunning brickwork, clapboard homes with gingerbread porches, big old trees and lush perennial gardens. A quick drive will take you to any of several beautiful parks along the lakeshore. A harbor of refuge was constructed in the 1970s, and there are plenty of slips in the marina, so if you're boating up the coast, take a side trip and discover Lexington.

If you're traveling with a small dog, you'll appreciate the pet-friendly policy here. Two rooms have been designed for well-behaved guest dogs. The Forest Room is particularly well suited because of its French doors leading to the outside patio and lawn.

Vitals

rooms: 5 with private baths

pets permitted: 2 rooms designated for well-behaved dogs

pets in residence: none

open season: year-round

rates: $105 to $120

e-mail: info@anighttorememberbandb.com

website: www.anighttorememberbandb.com

owners/innkeepers:
Nadine and Dan Maliniak
5712 Main Street
Lexington, MI 48450
810-359-7134

PLYMOUTH

932 Penniman

Kathy and Brian Susick had owned this gracious inn for about five hours when I first met them on a sunny fall day in 2012. Kathy had worked for a catering company for more than twenty years—a job that was flexible and fun and left her time for her family. Their Northville home was close to Plymouth, and they made frequent trips to the quaint city to go to the neighborhood movie theater ($3!) and attend free concerts in the park. They liked the restaurants there, too. And on one visit, when they were walking their little dog, they discovered 932 Penniman, a beautiful bed-and breakfast-inn that sits at the edge of downtown.

For Kathy's birthday, Brian booked a suite at the B&B, and over breakfast they learned that it was for sale. That's all Kathy needed to hear. "I love people and interacting with them," she said when I asked what attracted her to being an innkeeper. "It's the people—the guests!"

This large home was built in 1903 by a doctor, and it has classic Queen Anne details, plus arts and crafts touches and even some interesting neo-Gothic elements. It all comes together beautifully—the sunny bay windows, the honey-colored oak woodwork and pocket doors, the open oak staircase with hand-carved trim, built-in window seats and a deep wraparound porch.

In the late 1990s, the home was purchased and turned into a B&B. The owners did a fine job restoring and enhancing the structure, plus they added a perfectly matched two-story carriage house with two second-floor guest suites and a wonderful private, landscaped courtyard between the two buildings.

There are three guest rooms on the second floor of the home. I love the pencil-post four-poster bed in Linnea's Garden, and the queen-size sleigh bed and warm shades of yellow in Magnolia Maise. Rose Haven is a grand corner room flooded with light from four big windows and decorated in rich raspberry colors.

Plymouth rocks!

That's what they say in this vibrant little city, and it's been rocking for a long time. The first settlers here were Connecticut farmers William Starkweather and his wife Keziah, who purchased 240 acres from the US government on March 11, 1825, for $1.25 an acre. They built a rustic lean-to on what is now the southwest corner of Main Street and Ann Arbor Trail. It was later replaced with a log cabin.

Remember the Daisy BB gun? It got its start here. Plymouth inventor Clarence Hamilton introduced an idea to the Plymouth Iron Windmill Company in 1886: a metal and wire gunlike contraption that fired a lead ball using compressed air. The president of the company gave it a try, and, as history records, he said with enthusiasm, "Boy, that's a daisy!"

The name stuck, the guns were manufactured, and they became a premium that was given to farmers when they purchased a windmill. As things sometimes happen, the gun was such a huge success that the Plymouth Iron Windmill Company began manufacturing the Daisy BB gun in place of windmills, and the board of directors changed the name of the company to the Daisy Manufacturing Company, Inc.

Plymouth is built around Kellogg Park, which hosts dozens of events throughout the year, including the Plymouth Ice Spectacular. It's held on a weekend in January and is the largest and oldest ice-carving festival in North America.

Be sure to stop and see what's playing Thursday through Saturday at the town's beloved 1941 Penn Theater. It shows current second-run films plus classic and independent films, and it's managed by the nonprofit Friends of Penn. Rumor has it that the concession serves popcorn with real butter . . .

The two luxurious suites in the carriage house each have a gas fireplace with a seating area and a two-person whirlpool tub. The Tower Suite gets its name from the romantic turret that houses the tub. It also has a king-size bed. The Lodge Suite transports you to the Adirondacks with its queen-size log bed and touches of the north woods.

There are several areas for guests to enjoy on the first floor—in fact so many that you'll have plenty of opportunities to join other guests in conversation or find a quiet corner all to yourself. The Gathering Room, next to the dining room, has an original fireplace. There is an elegant Victorian parlor, and the three-season, glassed-in, wraparound porch has

great views of the grounds and Plymouth's charming downtown. Furnishings are a comfortable mix of antiques and traditional pieces with touches of contemporary arts and crafts. It's uncluttered, warm and very welcoming.

Breakfast is served in the formal dining room or, when weather permits, in the courtyard under the pergola. It's served between 9:00 and 9:30 a.m. on weekends and at whatever time best suits guests' needs on weekdays. Kathy is continuing the former innkeepers' tradition of serving a full plated meal with fruit, baked goods and hot entrées, and she's looking forward to developing her own specialties.

From 932 Penniman, it's an easy walk to Kellogg Park, which is the center of town, and to the restaurants, shops and movie theater that the Susicks have enjoyed so much over the years. Both Detroit Metropolitan Airport and the University of Michigan are about 30 minutes away.

Vitals

rooms: 5 rooms with private baths

pets permitted: no

pets in residence: 1 adorable small dog not allowed in guest rooms

open season: year-round

rates: $129 to $225

e-mail: innkeeper932@yahoo.com

website: www.bbonline.com/mi/penniman

owners/innkeepers:
   Kathy and Brian Susick
   932 Penniman Avenue
   Plymouth, MI 48170
   734-414-7444
   888-548-4887

YPSILANTI

The Parish House Inn

Ypsilanti is one of Michigan's oldest towns, and it has a lot going for it. There are more than a dozen well-maintained parks, which offer everything from bike paths and baseball diamonds to soccer fields, tennis courts, disc golf and picnic areas. Playgrounds and tot lots abound. Riverside Park encompasses nearly 14 acres in the center of the town, along the picturesque Huron River, and it has a fine fishing pier. Five-acre Frog Island Park, located in the Huron River, is connected to Riverside Park by a three-pointed bridge.

The city has one of the largest contiguous historic districts in the state, a vibrant downtown and scores of nineteenth-century homes. One of those homes is a Queen Anne built in 1893 to be the parsonage for the First Congregational Church. In 1987 it was moved about half a mile to Ypsilanti's historic district, where it sits today on a bluff high above the river. The back of the house was enlarged to include sleeping rooms plus a riverside main entrance that takes you into the breakfast room and kitchen. And that's where owner Chris Mason and I sat on a bright fall afternoon catching up and eating her warm-from-the-oven zucchini bread. Chris is a graduate of Washtenaw Community College's culinary arts program and the author of three cookbooks. Her most recent is *The Best of Breakfast Menus and Recipes.* She was hired to manage the bed and breakfast when it opened in 1993, and she bought it—all 5,300 square feet of it—in 1998.

Chris loves antiques, and she furnished the guest rooms with beautiful pieces plus elegant reproductions, vintage accessories and cozy quilts that complement the home's turn-of-the-century architecture. I am especially taken with the massive, hand-carved, mahogany four-poster bed in Room 4. Chris added a daybed to the room as well, making it perfect if you're traveling with a child or an extra friend. Room 3 has a king-size bed that can be made into twins. My favorite, Room 9, has

City on the river

A French Canadian fur trader from Montreal established a trading post in 1809 in the area now occupied by the town of Ypsilanti. In 1823 Major Thomas Woodruff established a permanent settlement on the on the east side of the Huron River, which was incorporated into the Territory of Michigan as Woodruff's Grove. Two years later another community developed on the west side of the river. It was called Ypsilantis after Demetrius Ypsilantis, a·hero in the Greek War of Independence. Woodruff's Grove changed its name to Ypsilantis in 1829, and the two communities merged a few years later. At some point, the s at the end was dropped, and no one seems to know why.

Michigan State Normal School, which became Eastern Michigan University, was founded in Ypsilanti in 1849. When the railroad came through in 1860 ferrying supplies and soldiers bound for the Civil War, hotels, bars and other businesses sprang up, and the area became known as Depot Town. Michigan's first interurban, the Ann Arbor and Ypsilanti Street Railway, began service in 1890, which must have delighted students at the Normal School, who were mostly young women, and the students at the University of Michigan, who were mostly young men.

Apex Motors produced the "ACE" car in Ypsilanti in 1920–22. Miller Motors Hudson opened here in 1929, and was the last Hudson dealership in the world. Preston Tucker designed and built the prototypes for his Tucker '48 here. Tom Monaghan, who founded Domino's Pizza, got his start in Ypsilanti with his DomiNick's Pizza.

---

a pretty iron king-size bed, a sleeper sofa, a corner table for two and a great view of the woods and river. All the rooms have cable TV, ceiling fans and air-conditioning. On the first floor, at the front of the house, are a parlor and dining room that can be used by small-group gatherings.

Guests often tell Chris that they don't normally take time to eat breakfast, but they do eat breakfast here! On the morning of my visit, they enjoyed omelets, potatoes, fresh-baked breads, fruit and juice. Sometimes Chris serves French toast or a quiche, baked oatmeal or pancakes. There are tables for two and four, so you can sit with other guests or take a spot by yourself. Guests also like Chris's "bottomless cookie jar." Along a wall in the breakfast room, you'll find a refrigerator and microwave oven for guests' to use, plus coffee and tea, popcorn and

cookies—always plenty of cookies. If you wake up in the middle of the night and you're hungry for something sweet, help yourself!

Chris says many of her guests stay at The Parish House while they are traveling for business, and in addition to her great breakfasts, they appreciate the comfort and special touches of her B&B. She has thoughtfully added a writing desk to each room, and if guests need space to spread out their work, they can use the second-floor parlor or the breakfast room tables. Outside the main entrance in the back is a garden patio, which overlooks the river far below. It's a lovely oasis, and I can imagine how nice it would be to relax there at the end of a busy day.

The Parish House is just a few blocks from downtown, so Chris encourages guests to leave their car at the inn and walk to the shops and restaurants nearby. You can also walk to Eastern Michigan University.

It's just a mile away. Ann Arbor is less than 10 minutes away by car. Detroit Metropolitan Airport is a 20-minute drive.

Vitals

rooms: 6 with private baths

pets permitted: no

pets in residence: none

rates: $99 to $150

open season: year-round

e-mail: parishinn@aol.com

website: parishhouseinn.com

owner/innkeeper:
Chris Mason
103 South Huron Street
Ypsilanti, MI 48197
734-480-4800
800-480-4866

Resources

Several associations and registries have been formed to promote Michigan's inns and bed-and-breakfast homes. Many set standards for members, conduct regular inspections and provide links to member websites. Check out the following for more information.

Michigan Lake to Lake Bed and Breakfast Association
This association was formed in 1983 and now represents more than 130 inns and bed-and-breakfast homes in both the Upper and Lower Peninsulas of Michigan. It is the largest association of B&Bs in Michigan and the only one with a statewide membership. Website: www.laketolake.com

Ludington Historic Bed and Breakfast Association
Website: www.ludingtonbedandbreakfast.com

Bed and Breakfast Inns of Michigan's Upper Peninsula
Website: www.upbnb.com

Southern Michigan Bed and Breakfast Association
Website: www.southernmichiganinns.com

State of Michigan's Pure Michigan promotion
Website: www.michigan.org/bed-breakfasts